Mastering Primary Art and Design

Mastering Primary Teaching series

Edited by Judith Roden and James Archer

The *Mastering Primary Teaching* series provides an insight into the core principles underpinning each of the subjects of the primary National Curriculum, thereby helping student teachers to 'master' the subjects. This in turn will enable new teachers to share this mastery in their teaching. Each book follows the same sequence of chapters, which has been specifically designed to assist trainee teachers to capitalize on opportunities to develop pedagogical excellence. These comprehensive guides introduce the subject and help trainees know how to plan and teach effective and inspiring lessons that make learning irresistible. Examples of children's work and case studies are included to help exemplify what is considered to be best and most innovative practice in primary education. The series is written by leading professionals, who draw on their years of experience to provide authoritative guides to the primary curriculum subject areas.

Also available in the series

Mastering Primary English, Wendy Jolliffe and David Waugh

Mastering Primary Design and Technology, Gill Hope

Mastering Primary Geography, Anthony Barlow and Sarah Whitehouse

Mastering Primary History, Karin Doull, Christopher Russell and Alison Hales

Mastering Primary Languages, Paula Ambrossi and Darnelle Constant-Shepherd

Mastering Primary Music, Ruth Atkinson

Mastering Primary Physical Education, Kristy Howells with Alison Carney, Neil Castle and Rich Little

Mastering Primary Religious Education, Maria James and Julian Stern

Mastering Primary Science, Amanda McCrory and Kenna Worthington

Forthcoming in the series

Mastering Primary Computing, Graham Parton

Also available from Bloomsbury

Developing Teacher Expertise, edited by Margaret Sangster

Readings for Reflective Teaching in Schools, edited by Andrew Pollard

Reflective Teaching in Schools, Andrew Pollard

Mastering Primary Art and Design

Peter Gregory, Claire March and Suzy Tutchell

BLOOMSBURY ACADEMIC
LONDON • NEW YORK • OXFORD • NEW DELHI • SYDNEY

BLOOMSBURY ACADEMIC
Bloomsbury Publishing Plc
50 Bedford Square, London, WC1B 3DP, UK
1385 Broadway, New York, NY 10018, USA
29 Earlsfort Terrace, Dublin 2, Ireland

BLOOMSBURY, BLOOMSBURY ACADEMIC and the Diana logo are trademarks
of Bloomsbury Publishing Plc

First published in Great Britain 2020
Reprinted 2021

Cover design: Anna Berzovan
Cover image © iStock (miakievy / molotovcoketail)

A catalogue record for this book is available from the British Library.

ISBN: HB: 978-1-4742-9490-4
PB: 978-1-4742-9487-4
ePDF: 978-1-4742-9491-1
eBook: 978-1-4742-9489-8

Series: Mastering Primary Teaching

Typeset by Deanta Global Publishing Service, Chennai, India
Printed and bound in Great Britain

To find out more about our authors and books visit www.bloomsbury.com and
sign up for our newsletters.

Contents

About the Authors

Peter Gregory has taught across all phases of education – leading subject development and curriculum design as well as undertaking local authority advisory work – and is currently Principal Lecturer in Education at Canterbury Christ Church University, UK, and regularly teaches and presents research across the UK, Europe and beyond. Now President of the National Society for Education in Art and Design (NSEAD), he was previously a World Councillor for the International Society for Education through Art (InSEA) and Chair of the Expert Subject Advisory Group (ESAG), which was originally set up by the Department for Education (DfE) to advise schools on the implementation of the 2013 National Curriculum. He is particularly interested in the development of highly effective teachers of Art and Design and ensuring their development through inspiring leadership in the subject, and he has written and contributed to several books, journals and other publications.

Claire March has been involved in making, problem-solving and creating in art ever since she can remember. As a teacher she combined her passion for art, design and teaching by leading the subject in primary schools in Kent, UK. Since working at Canterbury Christ Church University, UK, she has lectured on a number of programmes in Art and Design, covering the wider role of the Arts across the curriculum, as well as leading several projects with groups of schools. Her particular research interests relate to drawing and how children develop and use their personal journals or sketchbooks to develop their potential for self-expression.

Suzy Tutchell has a lifelong commitment and involvement in art education. Having been an art subject leader for many years in a variety of London-based primary schools, she moved on to advisory work as a creativity and early years consultant before working in higher education for the past ten years. As a lecturer, she currently leads the Art specialism on the primary BAEd programme at the University of Reading, UK. She is a practising artist whenever possible and continues to develop her own knowledge and identity as an artist/teacher.

Illustrations

Tables

Preface

We were very pleased to be asked to write this volume in the *Mastery of the National Curriculum* series. It seems to us that there are far too few opportunities for celebrating the possibilities of creation inside the primary classroom so we hope this book will inspire and inform readers as well as capture and convey our excitement in the subject of Art and Design.

There are three other things that we would like to set out at the beginning of the volume.

Firstly, our strong conviction that all primary aged children both can and should be able to develop and excel in Art and Design. In our work with students, as well as with teachers after they have qualified, we have experienced the closing of opportunities brought about not by a lack of talent, ability or understanding on the part of children, but rather by the limitations introduced and defined by those that have taught them. We have worked hard to deconstruct learned patterns of behaviour for which the foundations were laid, perhaps decades ago, by adults who did not know or had not experienced the liberation of the creative process. In their childhood classrooms, too many of our students encountered negative experiences, which conveyed that they weren't able to succeed. Today they need to re-engage with those experiences in order to develop into good teachers of Art and Design, and by doing so discover that their imagined limitations were all-too-often illusory. We would like to dedicate this book to those who are determined to find ways to ensure that all the children they will teach will not be limited but will enjoy the fullest and richest experiences imaginable. Surely the twenty-first century will need the creative thinking and leadership of these same primary pupils as they mature into adulthood.

Following from this conviction, we also want to give a fuller explanation of our understanding of the term 'mastery'. There are many who believe that it ought to convey a sense of elitism: that some learners will develop beyond the majority of their peers – probably due to the channelling of an innate ability through the training of an expert 'master'. By means of a staged hierarchy of knowledge and experience, the greater 'master' somehow selects and develops the talents of his or her pupils. In the light of what we have already expressed, we hope it will not come as a surprise that we are uncomfortable with this and reject the view. In fact, there are several good reasons for questioning such power relationships, as the sense of playfulness and experimentation in Art and Design can often render teacher and pupils alike as *collaborative* learners: both uncertain but both exploring ideas, materials and artworks with little sense of the likely outcome. The challenge of 'mastery' in this sense seems to us to relate more to the degree of confidence to be developed in, and then given, from those that teach. Our volume is produced in the hope that all teachers will find paths in mastery through its pages.

The final point relates to the appreciation we each have of community. We draw confidence from being a part of wider circles of professionals with interests in Art and Design and would want all primary teachers to similarly find such support and encouragement. We would like to commend the National Society for Education in Art and Design (NSEAD) as the best community of practice in the UK and the only combined subject association and learned society. NSEAD is a strong membership organization and welcomes members from all phases of education – yet it seems that many primary schools have suffered through the belief that individual teachers can develop a good level of art education on their own. As a consequence, many individual teachers and subject leaders have needlessly been isolated and unable to continue their own professional development. We would urge all those that read our volume to seek out the wider community of practice to which they not only belong but will also be able to contribute and allow other aspects of their mastery to be appreciated and honed. (Further details of NSEAD can be found at the end of the book.)

We hope that this volume contributes to both the present and future success of Art and Design in primary schools.

Peter Gregory, Claire March and Suzy Tutchell

Foreword

Bob and Roberta Smith

I am an artist. I understand that making art is about saying to the world, 'Look, I have made this … what do you think?'

Drawing images is a key part of language acquisition. Children draw a circle and say 'this is the cat'.

The good parent says 'Wow, so it is.'

And so a dialogical process between humans and images begins. All children are artists, just like all children are humanitarians – until the cynical adult world intervenes.

The opportunity for primary children to participate in the activities and thinking promoted and provoked by art, craft and design and all it can contribute to a broad and balanced curriculum, is essential. To respond to and celebrate a core message of the book, 'art is an irresistible activity'.

Alongside using, experimenting with and understanding the materials, tools, activities and techniques inherent in art, craft and design, time with the visual arts is time wisely invested in developing creativity, curiosity, asking questions, solving problems, the freedom to take risks, being vocal, initiating change and expressing feelings and ideas. The book acknowledges not only the need for and enjoyment of practical activities, but why we teach art, craft and design, which skills to start with, and, importantly, how these skills develop a child's autonomy.

Art, craft and design is a unique and essential element of everyone's education, especially in the primary phase. It is of immense importance to society that we activate the creativity within ourselves, not only to progress as artists to art school, but to be better problem-solvers, thinkers, mathematicians or scientists, and for our personal well-being and self-worth.

It cannot, however, be assumed that creativity miraculously happens when the paints and brushes come out. These unique experiences, vital to the development of visual literacy in every child, will not happen without the careful and considered pedagogical steps inherent in this excellent book. As a practising artist I believe in the value of the creative process and that the creative process and creative intent begins in childhood. It must be recognized and nurtured as a critical element in formal education.

What is happening globally now is complex; from climate change to geopolitics, from resource wars to how we teach, learn and work. Our children's futures are changing and unknown, our children need to be questioning and resilient, and art, craft and design in education will always develop and support that.

Alongside the value of art, craft and design in formal education, if we were to look back at the contribution of the creative, digital, cultural and heritage industries to our national and global economies we can see the creative capital we have gained. It is vital that this is recognized, celebrated and nurtured. For primary teachers of art, craft and design this book is a timely and essential guide and signpost.

Bob and Roberta Smith

Bob and Roberta Smith is the name of the British artist whose best known works include: *Make Art Not War*, which belongs to the Tate Collection and *Letter to Michael Gove*.

Bob and Roberta Smith studied for his MA at Goldsmiths from 1991 to 1993. He was an artist trustee of Tate between 2009 and 2013, and he is currently a trustee for the National Campaign for the Arts and a patron of NSEAD. He has recently been elected to be a Royal Academician.

Bob and Roberta Smith is actually one man. Before studying Fine Art at Goldsmiths in the early 1990s, Bob lived in Rome, New York and Wensleydale, and now lives between Leytonstone in East London and Ramsgate.

In 2013, Bob and Roberta launched the Art Party with Crescent Arts, Scarborough. The Art Party seeks to better advocate the arts to government. The Art Party is *not* a formal political party but is a loose grouping of artists and organizations who are deeply concerned about the way the government is diminishing the role of all the arts and design in schools.

Bob and Roberta Smith see art as an important element in democratic life. Much of his art takes the form of painted signs. Central to Bob and Roberta Smith's thinking is the idea that campaigns are extended artworks that include a variety of consciousness raising artefacts.

Figure 0.1 Through our art (Bob and Roberta Smith)

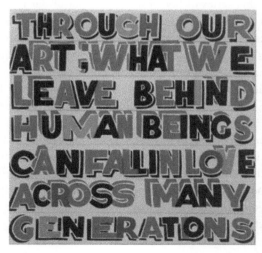

Series Editors' Foreword

A long and varied experience of working with beginner and experienced teachers in primary schools has informed this series since its conception. Over the last thirty years there have been many changes in practice in terms of teaching and learning in primary and early years education. Significantly, since the implementation of the first National Curriculum in 1989 the aim has been to bring best practice in primary education to all state schools in England and Wales. As time has passed, numerous policy decisions have altered the detail and emphasis of the delivery of the primary curriculum. However, there has been little change in the belief that pupils in the primary and early years phases of education should receive a broad, balanced curriculum based on traditional subjects.

Recent Ofsted subject reports and notably the *Cambridge Primary Review* indicate that rather than the ideal being attained, in many schools the emphasis on English and mathematics has not only depressed the other subjects of the primary curriculum, but also narrowed the range of strategies used for the delivery of the curriculum. The amount of time allocated to subject sessions in initial teacher education (ITE) courses has dramatically reduced, which may also account for this narrow diet in pedagogy.

The vision for this series of books was borne out of our many years of experience with student teachers. As a result, we believe that the series is well designed to equip trainee and beginner teachers to master the art of teaching in the primary phase. This series of books aims to introduce current and contemporary practices associated with the whole range of subjects within the Primary National Curriculum and religious education. It also goes beyond this by providing beginner teachers with the knowledge and understanding required to achieve mastery of each subject. In doing so, each book in the series highlights contemporary issues, such as assessment and inclusion, which are the key areas that even the most seasoned practitioner is still grappling with in light of the introduction of the new Primary Curriculum. In agreement with the results attached with these books, we believe that students who work in schools and progress to newly qualified teacher (NQT) status will be able to make a significant contribution to the provision in their school, especially in foundation subjects.

Readers will find great support within each one of these books. Each book in the series will inform and provide the opportunity for basic mastery of each of the subjects, namely English, mathematics, science, physical education, music, history, geography, design and technology, computing and religious education. They will discover the essence of each subject in terms of its philosophy, knowledge and skills. Readers will also be inspired by the enthusiasm for each subject revealed by the subject authors who are experts in their field. They will discover many and varied strategies for making each subject 'come alive' for their pupils and they should become more confident about teaching across the whole range of subjects represented in the primary and early years curriculum.

Primary teaching in the state sector is characterized by a long history of pupils being taught the whole range of the primary curriculum by one teacher. Although some schools may employ specialists to deliver some subjects of the curriculum, notably physical education, music or science, for example, it is more usual for the whole curriculum to be delivered to a class by their class teacher. This places a potentially enormous burden on beginner teachers no matter which route they use to enter teaching. The burden is especially high on those entering through employment-based routes and for those who aim to become inspiring primary teachers. There is much to learn!

The term 'mastery' is generally considered to relate to knowledge and understanding of a subject that incorporates the 'how' of teaching as well as the 'what'. Although most entrants to primary teaching will have some experience of the primary curriculum as a pupil, very few will have experienced the breadth of the curriculum or have any understanding of the curriculum, which reflects recent trends in teaching and learning within the subject. The primary curriculum encompasses a very broad range of subjects, each of which has its own knowledge base, skills and ways of working. Unsurprisingly, very few new entrants into the teaching profession hold mastery of all the interrelated subjects. Indeed for the beginner teacher it may well be many years before full mastery of all aspects of the primary curriculum can be achieved. The content of the primary curriculum has changed significantly, notably in some foundation subjects, such as history and music. So although beginner teachers might hold fond memories of these subjects from their own experience of primary education, the content of the subject may well have changed significantly over time and may incorporate different emphases.

This series, *Mastering Primary Teaching*, aims to meet the needs of those who, reflecting the desire for mastery over each subject, want to know more. This is a tall order. Nevertheless, we believe that the pursuit of development should always be rewarded, which is why we are delighted to have so many experts sharing their well-developed knowledge and passion for the subjects featured in each book. The vision for this series is to provide support for those who are beginning their teaching career, who may not feel fully secure in their subject knowledge, understanding and skill. In addition, the series also aims to provide a reference point for beginner teachers to always be able to go back to support them in the important art of teaching.

Intending primary teachers, in our experience, have a thirst for knowledge about the subjects that they will be teaching. They want to 'master' new material and ideas in a range of subjects. They aim to gain as much knowledge as they can of these subjects, in some of which the beginner teachers may lack confidence, or may be scared of, because of their perceived lack of familiarity with certain subjects and particularly how they are delivered in primary schools. Teaching the primary curriculum can be one of the most rewarding experiences. We believe that this series will help the beginner teachers to unlock the primary curriculum in a way that ensures they establish themselves as confident primary practitioners.

Judith Roden
James Archer

How to Use this book

This book is one of twelve books that together help form a truly innovative series aimed to support your development. Each book follows the same format and chapter sequence. There is an emphasis throughout the book on providing information about the teaching and learning of Art and Design. You will find a wealth of information within each chapter that will help you to understand the issues, problems and opportunities that teaching the subject can provide you as a developing practitioner in the subject. Crucially, each chapter provides opportunities for you to reflect upon important points linked to your development in order that you may develop your confidence in and master the teaching of Art and Design. There really is something for everyone within each chapter.

Each chapter has been carefully designed to help you to develop your knowledge of the subject systematically and as a result contains key features. Chapter objectives clearly signpost the content of each chapter and these will help you to familiarize yourself with important aspects of the subject and will orientate you in preparation for reading the chapter. The regular 'pause for thought' points offer questions and activities for you to reflect on important aspects of the subject. Each pause for thought provides you with an opportunity to enhance your learning beyond merely reading the chapter. These will sometimes ask you to consider your own experience and what you already know about the teaching of the subject. Others will require you to critique aspects of good practice presented as case studies or research. To benefit fully from reading this text, you need to be an active participant. Sometimes you are asked to make notes on your responses to questions and ideas and then to revisit these later on in your reading. While it would be possible for you to skip through the opportunities for reflection, or to give only cursory attention to the questions and activities that aim to facilitate deeper reflection than might otherwise be the case, we strongly urge you to engage with the pause for thought activities. It is our belief that it is through these moments that most of your transformational learning that will occur as a result of engaging with this book.

We passionately believe that learners of all ages learn best when they work with others, so we would encourage you, if possible, to work with another person, sharing your ideas and perspectives. The book also would be ideal for group study within a university or school setting.

This book has been authored by Peter Gregory, Claire March and Suzy Tutchell, who are experienced and highly regarded as professionals in their subject area. They are strong voices within the primary art and design community. By reading this book you will be able to benefit from their rich knowledge, understanding and experience. When using this book, ensure that you are ready to learn from some of the greats in primary art and design.

Acknowledgements

As a team we would like to acknowledge all the energy that has been invested in producing this book: Chapters 1, 2 and 7 were drafted by Peter, Chapters 4, 5 and 8 by Claire and Chapters 3 and 6 by Suzy. The final edit was undertaken by Peter.

We are very grateful to the children, parents, teachers and artists who have given their permission to allow us to share their photographs and their examples of artworks.

We would specifically like to acknowledge:

The children and staff from a number of schools: Aston Fence J&I School, Sheffield; Birch Copse Primary School, Reading; Caol Primary School, Fort William; Grinling Gibbons Primary School, Deptford; Halstow Primary School, Greenwich; Hawkinge Primary School, Folkestone; Loddon Primary School, Reading; Millennium Primary School, Greenwich; Minster-in-Sheppey Primary School, Sheppey; New Hinksey Primary School, Oxford; Oxford Road Community Primary School, Reading; Palm Bay Primary School, Thanet; River Primary School, Dover; St Ebbes Primary School, Oxford; St Eanswythes CE Primary School, Dover; St Mary's Dover CE Primary School, Dover; St Mary Magdelene CE School, Woolwich; Westdale Junior School, Nottingham; Wood Fold Primary School, Wigan; Woodchurch CE Primary, Woodchurch.

The galleries and other spaces in which the artworks have been exhibited: Canterbury Christ Church University; Deptford market; Folkestone Triennial; Samphire Hoe, Dover; Turner Contemporary, Margate; and University of Reading.

The student teachers from: University of Reading: Y2 BA Ed Primary Education, Y1 and Y2 BA Ed Art specialists; Canterbury Christ Church University: Y2 BA Primary Education Art and Design specialists, PGCE and Enhanced Studies students; University of Winchester: PGCE students; University of Greenwich: Y3 BA Primary Education Art and Design specialists.

The lecturers and tutors at the IoE, University of Reading and Canterbury Christ Church University and **the artist colleagues** who have supported the development of the book – especially Sharon Witt, Maria Vinney, Gill Hopper, Natasha Morland and Sue Shaw.

Our very patient and supportive families – especially Maia and Joel Thomas (and their willing friends), Lyn and Elana.

Our deep appreciation to all the children and students who continue to inspire our own practice, thinking and learning in art and education.

We especially would like to thank Bob and Roberta Smith, Sioux Peto, Matt Rowe, Lucy Matthew, Jo Human and Hannah Yasson for allowing us to use their photographs as well as Graham Jennings, Dan China and Caleb Simmons for their help with diagrams.

Lastly, we would like to dedicate this book to everyone from whom we have learned so much and in appreciation for their help and support that has been given to us throughout our writing and editing of this book.

Chapter 1
An Introduction to Primary Art and Design

This chapter deals with the rather basic but incredibly important questions:

- What is primary Art and Design?
- Why should it be taught?
- What does it mean to be artistic and how does this link to the curriculum subject?
- How can Art and Design contribute to a child's whole education?

Without a good understanding of these issues, we would argue there is a very strong likelihood of building activities in the classroom that simply do not enrich children's experiences in the short term or provide a robust framework for growing artistic endeavour for recreation, employment or creative industry in the longer term. Before we begin to unpick each question, it would be useful to briefly consider the current statutory expectations for the subject in the context of the journey to the current time.

Quick pause moment – *Think about the value of Art and Design in education*:

- What do you think is the point of Art and Design as a school subject?
- What do think that children learn from studying Art and Design?
- How would you explain to a child *why* we are doing Art and Design in class today?

An introduction to primary Art and Design

Prior to the introduction of the National Curriculum, primary education embraced the subject we would today refer to as 'Art and Design' in a number of ways. Firstly, from Victorian times, the subject of 'drawing' was considered fundamental to a well-rounded education. It often reflected the classical approach to reproducing a likeness of reality by drawing a range of objects from different angles. The linkage with geometric elements of mathematics was always acknowledged but the importance of children being taught to observe closely also related to the making of objects in the future. There are many who forget that the fourth 'R' in traditional education referred to 'routing' – the act of creating things. Without this, the place of drawing is often relegated to a position of lesser importance in our minds today.

After the Second World War, the creative processes of art were regarded as important to allow humanity to both explore and define the avenues of hope for the future. It was with this in mind that people like Herbert Read and Marion Richardson argued strongly for increasing the place of art in the primary curriculum. They understood art as being more than drawing and even more than simply reproducing observed artefacts. The art world across the twentieth century had increasingly explored other forms and the now-famous artists like Pablo Picasso, Georges Braque, Hannah Höch, Salvador Dali, Georgia O'Keefe, Cornelia Parker and many others besides, have caused this thinking to be interwoven into mainstream art. The so-called 'child art' movement applied the thinking to children and the notion that children themselves could be artists in their own right increasingly affected the practice in many classrooms (Macdonald, 2004). All of these influences resulted in the birth of the International Society for Education through Art under the aegis of the United Nations Educational, Scientific and Cultural Organization (UNESCO).

By the time of the Plowden Report in 1967, art was a major component of learning in primary schools. It was not at all uncommon for many art processes to be taught and explored at the same time in the classroom. There was little expectation of a defined curriculum to be covered and the importance of actually making art was reflected throughout all the subjects studied. Art at this time was seen as an activity rather than a lesson of received instruction (Lancaster, 1987). Most primary schools engaged in significant art-based activities throughout the academic year for pupils of all ages but this was set to change dramatically as teachers 'were challenged by the emergence and demands of the new national curriculum' (Clement and Tarr, 1992: 1).

The first National Curriculum for England was born in 1989 and although art was a planned subject within the suite of subjects that schools were required to teach, its official programme of study (Department of Education and Science (DES), 1992) was not published until 1992 – following after the 'core' subjects and starting the reinforcement of a different hierarchy of subjects. As a consequence, art was about to slip in importance in many teachers' minds.

In common with all of the subjects of the early National Curriculum, the material to be taught was set out in an A4 ring binder. This contained both the statutory content and non-statutory guidance to help teachers appreciate what it meant and the links that might be helpful to make in their teaching (DES, 1992). The complete library of folders meant that classroom teachers were bound to struggle to cover all the curriculum and within a short space of time there were calls for a new 'slimmed down' curriculum.

A revised version was published in 1995 (only three years after the first version of the art curriculum). Art continued to be defined, but there was less content and a stronger message about the importance of the core subjects (Department for Education (DfE), 1995). Many schools struggled with the core subjects, and the early

Ofsted reports underlined the desirability of reconceptualizing the curriculum structure in order to give the core subjects the dominance that politicians required. The 1995 curriculum was replaced in 1999.

The so-called millennium version of the National Curriculum (Qualifications and Curriculum Authority (QCA), 1999) brought together aspects of the previous versions: there was a single compendium document that presented all of the subjects, together with other aspects – including an inclusion statement and the underlying values of education. Art was now retitled 'Art and Design' and the importance of graphic design was made very explicit. The breadth of the subject included photography, architecture, digital media and artworks from other cultures. Seemingly in fewer words, the subject had been presented clearly for teachers.

The relentless dominance of the core subjects continued. So much so, that a counterwave arguing for the importance of creativity and the arts was led by a rare example of joined-up thinking from the (then) Department for Education and the Department for Sport, Media and Culture. The very insightful *All Our Futures* report (DfE, 1999) even argued that the distinction between 'core' and 'foundation' subjects was unhelpful and ought to be abandoned. This recommendation was not enacted but several other developments to further promote creativity were commissioned.

By the end of the first decade of the twenty-first century, there was widespread agreement that a new form of curriculum structure was needed. Two different studies were commissioned: the first, frequently known as the Cambridge Primary Review, was an independent review (Alexander, 2010), which claimed to be bigger and more thorough than the earlier Plowden Report almost forty years earlier. The second was commissioned by the government of the day and was referred to as the Rose Review. It was this that gave rise to an altogether different curriculum document in 2010 (Department for Children, Schools and Families (DCSF), 2010). This built a structure around six areas of learning (similar but not identical to the Early Years Curriculum Framework) and unashamedly presented the contents not in subject domains but in cross-curricular groups. The 'Expressive Arts' section set out some simple connecting structures in the curriculum but largely left teachers to define the topics that they taught themselves. The political events of 2010 meant that although the new National Curriculum document was printed and despatched to schools, parliament failed to allow sufficient time for debating it before a general election took place. The new, incoming government decided not to adopt this version but set about defining another of its own.

In 2013, the most recent version of the Art and Design curriculum (DfE, 2013) was published. Many objected to the wording, the overly simplified statements and points of contradiction contained within it. Very little change was effected during consultation and the contents refer to materials, techniques, knowledge and skills almost interchangeably. The subject was reduced to two sides of A4 text and, sadly, many schools have failed to notice that it is impossible to achieve the aims of the subject simply by tackling each bullet point in turn. The consequence for the subject in primary schools is less than desirable. We would like to point readers in the direction of an annotated and expanded version of the DfE document, produced by the National Society for Education in Art and Design (NSEAD, 2014), which can be freely downloaded from the website. This version tries to make sure that all teachers can understand what was meant by the official one and uses a broad interpretation of the subject to do so. (There is also an accompanying glossary for those who are unfamiliar with the technical terminology of the subject.)

So, having briefly considered the historical development of the subject we know as 'Art and Design', we would like to turn the readers' attention to the ways in which their understanding and execution in their classrooms will determine its success throughout the twenty-first century and beyond.

What is primary Art and Design?

As already noted, the understanding of the school subject domain is more than a little related to the subject as known, understood and experienced in the wider world context. 'Drawing' developed into 'art' then 'Art and Design' – but the fuller explanation that the subject should be interpreted as 'art, craft and design' (used by Lancaster in 1987 has only been provided in the small print of the National Curriculum since 1999). As artworks produced today may sometimes embrace concepts concerning skill, utilize non-visual forms (e.g. sound), or quickly adopt and subvert new media (e.g. 3D, drawing or printing techniques), there isn't likely to be a simple singular definition that will cover all eventualities of the forms produced. The challenge for educators is whether our own understanding will limit and restrict the art that we teach and expose our pupils to – or whether our own thinking will remain flexible, adapting and thus allowing all art forms to be represented under the title of the subject domain.

Looking at the published literature, there are several ways of tackling the question. Wilson (2005) and Gopaul (2017), for instance, both offer a number of material processes from which to judge the spread of opportunities incorporated into the experiences offered in the primary school. These include: drawing (including observational drawing), painting, printmaking, collage, textiles and 3D work. Hewlett and March (2016) refer to a similar spread but they also begin to point to the boundaries of the materials themselves, as many teachers feel unable to tackle all but instead focus on a limited range – usually reflecting the range that they have experienced themselves. It has also been noted that primary school teachers may have insufficient understanding of art to be able to teach it well (Downing and Johnson, 2003) and they may concentrate on those areas where they feel more confident. These limitations then are more likely to be encountered by the expectations of the teachers rather than through the definitions of the curriculum documents. Tutchell (2014) argued for greater focus on the creativity within the subject domain, rather than simply repeating the material processes. More recently, Ogier (2017) suggested it was time to move away from a simple definition of the subject and ordered her book around themes affecting the pedagogical elements for teachers. The section on processes and practice still

Figures 1.1 and 1.2 Different art forms (felt craft and pen-and-ink drawing)

referred to the same material processes but added 'Craftwork and making' as well as 'New media and technology' (2017: 65–136). (See Figures 1.1 and 1.2.) All in all, Ian Middleton, at that time the specialist Her Majesty's Inspector (HMI) for Art and Design (in Wilson, 2005) summed it up as:

> a broad, balanced and creative approach … which stimulates and builds on pupil's art skills, knowledge and understanding … [providing] a very helpful framework for primary schools [and] … essential reference for secondary schools making appropriate provision to capitalise on pupil's enjoyment and experience.
>
> Middleton (2005: v)

From these various perspectives, we can start to observe both the commonly agreed parameters of the subject domain and also the points of tension where the subject itself is providing areas of challenge for teachers. It is because of these that the depth of understanding set out in this volume is particularly important. It is relatively easy to outline a series of activities that could be organized and provided in a primary classroom. It is far harder to work within a more fluid and developing model of what the subject domain is today – or even what it might become tomorrow. We would like to suggest in this volume that it is in this depth of understanding that the mastery of the subject can now be detected in classrooms across the land. Where a single perspective of, say, aesthetics, is understood to require pupils' responses to the offered interpretations of beauty, the learners are narrowed and potentially misled in their art education. We are convinced that where teachers can grasp and articulate other contemporary perspectives, including those of shock, intrigue and curiosity, they will better prepare their pupils for the requirements of the National Curriculum, the creative processes and indeed the possibilities of employment in adult life as well. This brings us to a new challenge: exactly what is going on in the teaching of Art and Design in primary classrooms? And how do we know?

> ## Quick pause moment – *Write down your thoughts before going on*:
>
> - How would you now define Art and Design?
> - What would you want the children in your class to experience in the subject?

What is happening in primary classrooms today?

The reader might be somewhat surprised to hear that actually there is very little evidence available for us to present the answers to these questions. Gregory (2017a) outlined the paucity of research – based evidence from which to distil such an understanding. In the early part of the twenty-first century, Ofsted inspectors regularly inspected the subject in schools and turned their attention to current practices and where aspects were being missed. The last two subject survey inspections (Ofsted, 2009 and 2012) presented an educational landscape almost unrecognizable from the earlier sources (see above, p. 3). By 2012, the inspectors noted that the majority of primary schools failed to enable pupils to achieve the levels of which they were capable and, even more worryingly, they noted that the quality of teaching was less than good in the same proportion of schools. There is little to suggest that things have improved since that time, as other external factors are likely to have weakened the situation even further – loss of Local Authority support, reduction in continuing professional development in the subject, reductions in the time given to Art and Design in initial teacher education, and the demands on time for other curriculum subjects (NSEAD, 2016; Gregory, 2017b).

Within the list of aspects that remain unknown, there are some areas that are still unexplored and ought to challenge art educators looking for opportunities for research:

- the varieties of art curriculum planned and actually taught in classes;
- allocation of teaching time to the subject;
- contemporary primary art pedagogies and how they are applied;
- correlations between teachers' personal histories and pupils' experiences of being taught;
- larger-scale research (including longitudinal studies);
- ways of strengthening the training of teachers in Art and Design;
- measuring pupils' progress and achievement in art; and
- use of new media and art practices.

To summarize, there is no one definition of what art is – or isn't – that conveniently draws all content together into a single list. What is believed by teachers will affect

Figure 1.3 KS1 printing/drawing

what is actually taught, and the importance of experience gained by them seems to affect their understanding. In the pages of this book, we will refer to the very best practices in Art and Design and offer these for consideration, reflection and investment.

Why should the subject of 'Art and Design' be taught?

There are several justifications for the variety of answers to this question as well. The current National Curriculum (DfE, 2013: 1) suggests a few, indicating that it will:

- engage, inspire and challenge pupils' thinking;
- allow children to think critically and develop a more rigorous understanding of the subject;
- equip children with the knowledge and skills to experiment, invent and create their own works; and
- enable children to know how the subject both reflects and shapes our history as well as the contribution it makes to the culture, creativity and wealth of the nation.

This seems a far cry from the earlier comments about reinforcing a view of the subject by a particular teacher or group of adults as already noted (although it must be noted that there is little in this list about the preparation it will offer for either the children's future or for the future of the global community). The extent to which the subject is able to achieve all these does seem to rest on the understanding and experience of the teachers. In schools where the subject is well taught, we would suggest that there will be a vibrant, constant delight in the challenges implicit within it. But there are other justifications that it would be helpful to consider too.

Elliott Eisner listed ten things that the arts teach as a means of understanding the benefit for including them in our classrooms:

- Children are taught to make good judgements about qualitative relationships. (Unlike much of the curriculum in which correct answers and rules prevail, in the arts subjects, it is judgment rather than rules that prevail.)
- Children can discover that problems can have more than one solution and that questions can have more than one answer.
- Through the subject, children can celebrate multiple perspectives. (One of their fundamental lessons is that there are many ways to see and interpret the world.)
- Children engage in complex forms of problem-solving, where purposes are seldom fixed but change with circumstance and opportunity. (Learning in the arts requires the ability and a willingness to surrender to the unanticipated possibilities of the work as it unfolds.)
- The subject vividly makes the fact that neither words in their literal form nor numbers exhaust what we can know. (The limits of our language do not define the limits of our cognition.)
- Students learn that small differences can have large effects. (The arts traffic in subtleties.)
- Students are encouraged to think through and within a material. (All art forms employ some means through which images become real.)
- The subject helps children learn to say what cannot be said. (When children are invited to disclose what a work of art helps them feel, they must reach into their poetic capacities to find the words that will do the job.)
- The subject enables us all to have experiences that we can have from no other source and through such experience to discover the range and variety of what we are capable of feeling.
- The subject's position in the school curriculum symbolises to the young what adults believe is important.

Eisner, 2002: 72

From both these lists, there are several common aspects that we will seek to develop throughout this book.

We do not understand Art and Design as a fixed subject, and it requires (even demands) the investment and application of deep thinking, which utilizes and affects our cognitive abilities. Through these intellectual processes, we understand and make sense of the world – including our times and experiences – but also more broadly of humanity itself (including those who have preceded us and those who may follow us). It both carries values and allows us a range of lenses through which we can detect and examine those values. It is absorbing and fully engages us – our intellect, our emotions and even our spirituality. The extent to which Art and Design allows such views to be grasped will determine the ways that the children in our schools develop as critical consumers and producers in contemporary society and, later, as adults in the years to come.

Looking across the present range of National Curriculum subjects, it is hard to imagine such claims being made by most of the other domains. And yet, Art and Design is too often misunderstood and misrepresented as being of little consequence.

The enormity of these aspects of the subject may overwhelm some readers. Their past experience may have been too fragile or restrictive, but they ought not to worry as we are deliberately attempting to provoke thinking around what might be taught in primary classrooms and the justifications for doing so.

Herne (in Cox and Watts, 2007: 6) listed eight reasons why he felt Art and Design occupied a unique place in the primary curriculum:

- It offers children opportunities to develop a range of skills, techniques and practices, some of which date back centuries while others are contemporary in nature.

- It is a unique visual and tactile language with a set of elements that can be combined to make possible powerful visual statements.

- Through developing as artists, designers and critics, children can develop skills that make them 'visually literate', learning about ways of interpreting and responding works of art.

- It offers potential for individual expression that satisfies a human need to communicate; this can provide deep satisfaction and promote mental balance and well-being.

- A core of observation work can provide a study skill, training in precise looking, concentration and visual and tactile sensitivity.

- It develops an understanding of the creative processes, which is highly valued, not only in itself, but also as a transferable skill in contemporary life and work.

- Being introduced to art and culture with a global perspective develops cultural awareness, sensitivity and appreciation of diversity (sometimes called 'cultural literacy').

- Practical art activity and critical response to artists' work develop intellectual and aesthetic awareness and design skills that are worthwhile in themselves as well as useful in everyday life and employment.

We would like to commend all three lists above (DfE, 2013; Eisner, 2002; Herne, 2007) for reflection: between them, they form the basis of what lies ahead in this book. Their importance fuels our drive, passion and concern to provoke others to develop the learning of children in Art and Design.

Quick pause moment – *A scenario-based question*:

- You have just been awarded a large sum of money for equipment, materials and resources to enhance the provision for your class. What will you buy for Art and Design and why?

What does it mean to be artistic and how does this link to the curriculum subject?

It might be tempting to oversimplify the idea of being artistic as demonstrating the traits and attributes of artists. This severely limits the meaning of the term and may have other undesirable effects. (For example, there are several studies that demonstrate that children often receive a transmitted idea that artists are predominantly male.) Our view is that every individual human is artistic so this idea needs to be deconstructed further if our position is to be understood and applied well in the context of the curriculum subject.

Too often we have been told by reluctant student teachers that they aren't artistic. This usually has meant that they have been trained to hold a view that artistic means a particular way of reproducing images (often but not exclusively by drawing), and they have been persuaded that they don't have this ability. We have noted that there can be a form of collusion between the teachers from such a student's past and their view of themselves. As teachers we bear a huge responsibility for the effect we have on the pupils we encounter. This can be detected in the ways some adults are prepared to think of themselves, as their negative descriptions indicate a very limiting impact on their identity: 'I can't, therefore I become someone who can't.' This impacts their view of artistry (and, we would add, their understanding of mastery in Art and Design).

To be artistic is to have confidence in the processes of making art. We may have stronger experiences and talents with some forms than with others, but there needs to be an underlying confidence on which to build. In the average primary classroom of thirty pupils, about three pupils in each class will grow up to work in the creative industries (Creative Industries Federation, 2018) – although this is built on our

Figure 1.4 An opportunity to visit a gallery

current employment realities. In the future, there is likely to be a greater requirement for confident artistic thinkers to develop those industries even further.

Looking again above at the reasons why art is taught, it is clear that the development of the artistic traits of humanity is a crucial thread. This poses some new challenges for us. It would be very easy to fall into the trap of conveying art that has only been made by Europeans – whereas art has been made wherever people have been or are to be found. The reinforcement of certain materials – for example, painting on paper or canvas – is equally unhelpful and we ought to acknowledge that much art produced over the millennia has been added to rock or wood, for example. The embracing of technology has been instrumental to these processes, sometimes by appropriating developments in ways that had not necessarily been intended.

Probably the easiest examples of such appropriation can be seen in the development of painting techniques in the latter part of the eighteenth century. The Impressionist movement is associated with impressions of colour and texture applied with brushstrokes applied by courageous artists who broke with traditions of painting in certain predictable ways. Why did they do this? Was it that they were rebellious and 'artistic'? Actually this doesn't quite provide a full explanation. There were three important technological influences on their practice. The first was the coming of age of photography. (It had been developed over the previous forty years before it 'freed' the Impressionist painters from the need to record with a photographic precision.) The second was a growing awareness of the forms of impressions that might be seen from moving transport: the age of the steam train meant more people travelled using this form of transport. Thirdly, and some might say most importantly, the development of metal tubes to house ready-mixed pigments in the form of paints allowed these painters to work outside ('*en plein aire*') rather than make many sketches and build a painting from them back in their studios.

Figures 1.5 and 1.6 KS2 collage and sculptural form

 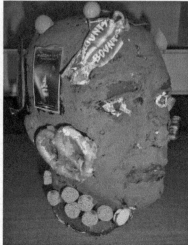

The age of artistic education is far from over. In primary schools today, pupils could be taught about digital photography, animation production, image manipulation (using Photoshop or similar software) or drawing in 3D using the new stylus technology (before moving to 3D printing). We say they *could* because the reality will depend on the teachers' ability to embrace these newer forms and whether or not they recognize the artistry demanded within them, as well as whether they see these *as* actual art forms as well. So much depends on these rather fragile connections. Much of this book is therefore devoted to demonstrating how these can be made, strengthened and sustained.

How can Art and Design contribute to a child's whole education?

In our discussions so far, we have already acknowledged the complexity of learning processes in Art and Design. We have seen the developmental processes that the subject either directly supports or that may enhance the development of well-rounded, balanced and creative individuals.

This view is not new, Vygotsky (1972), Dewey (1934), Read (1948), Eisner (2002) and Gardner (1990) have all demonstrated powerful arguments for considering such perspectives. Although we will not explore their thinking in great detail here, we would recommend the curious readers do so for themselves and reflect on their own childhood experiences together with their hopes for those that they teach today.

In the preface to his picture book *The Artist who Painted a Blue Horse*, Eric Carle, the well-known children's illustrator, recalls the impact that his art teacher had upon

Figure 1.7 Inspiring teachers

him, encouraging him to view the artworks of Franz Marc (Carle, 2013). This was done at considerable risk, as the artworks had been forbidden by the Nazi government and were not supposed to be mentioned in school. The impact on his life, learning experiences and his own art was considerable. Without this episode, there might not have been a very hungry caterpillar in the lives of many other children! Many others refer to specific episodes in their own development (including Hickman, 2011 and Gregory, 2016) and the sense of inspiration and encouragement invested in them by their teachers becomes an inspiration in itself.

We hope that this book will find its way into the hearts of many primary teachers of Art and Design and that the legacy of many earlier art educators continues. The following chapters will consider the importance of inspiring learning and the ways that this might be achieved in Art and Design.

Quick pause moment – *Think about how you inspire your pupils*:

- What art, craft and design activities do you do yourself? How could you share your experiences to motivate, engage, encourage and inspire your pupils?
- Reflect on your answers before moving on.

Recommended reading

The following three texts are suggested as follow-on reading:

Herne, S. (2007), 'The Subject of Art and Design', in S. Cox and R. Watts (eds), *Teaching Art and Design 3–11* London: Continuum, pp. 1–8.

Hewlett, C. and March, C. (2016), 'An Introduction to Art and Design', in P. Driscoll, A. Lambirth and J. Roden (eds), *The Primary Curriculum: A Creative Approach*, 2nd ed. London: Sage, pp. 176–94.

Ofsted. (2012), *Making a Mark: Art, Craft and Design in Schools (2008–11)*. London: Ofsted.

Chapter 2
Current Developments in Art and Design

Introduction

In the earlier pages, we established that the monitoring processes of Art and Design by the Office for Standards in Education, Children's Services and Skills (Ofsted) have ceased, with the last subject survey report being published in 2012. This could be viewed as a disastrous position, with concerns that since that time nothing more is known or has been developed without Ofsted's leadership. In this chapter we will examine the actual circumstances in more detail and reflect on the present situation and the impact that this has (or may have) on Art and Design in the primary school.

In this chapter we will consider:

- The current state of primary Art and Design?
- The external view.
- The place of research in Art and Design education.
- What does the research actually say?
- How can teachers positively contribute to children's enjoyment of Art and Design?
- The choices ahead.

Quick pause moment – *Thinking* again *about the value of Art and Design in education*:

- What do you think is happening in Art and Design in primary schools?
- How confident are you in identifying high quality Art and Design being taught?
- Where would you turn for further guidance?

What is the current state of primary Art and Design?

As we consider the big picture of Art and Design in schools today, what sources of evidence do you think will be most useful? Too often teachers can be isolated and unaware of what is happening outside their own classrooms so this is a very pertinent question. There are a number of possible sources, these include the information gleaned from learning walks around the school, honest discussions between teachers in local network groups and communities, online reflections, inspection reports and what might be broadly termed 'research'. All of these will be useful to some extent, but there is an important underlying issue: which sources can be relied upon as indicators of contemporary good practice and which might just be reinforcing activities that happen today?

Learning walks can be a really useful way of understanding the subject as it is treated and valued within a school setting. They are commonly used for core subjects but less so for Art and Design – to the frustration of many subject leaders. Careful looking could reveal the spread of media and techniques across the different year groups. It could also point towards aspects of progress expected, ignored or celebrated. There is likely to be an illustrated list of artists studied – with all the limitations and concerns already noted in the first chapter and elsewhere in this book. Learning walks could also involve fresh pairs of eyes in the form of interested third parties. Governors could take an interest in the work of the school and ask to join staff (for suggestions of joint activities refer to National Society for Education in Art and Design (NSEAD)/Arts Council, 1332017). Pupils from different key stages or members of the art club could also add to this alternative perspective. (See Figure 2.1.)

Figure 2.1 Learning walks can reveal useful insights into teaching and learning

So far, we have referred to a number of possibilities but the majority of primary teachers that we speak to have never been on such a learning walk nor have they been encouraged to do so. The very keen teachers find a lively community of others with an interest in the subject. In this way, they can share their skills, inspirations and experiences. There are a number of online communities – including that of NSEAD – where similar activities take place. But how can we be sure that what is shared is more than enthusiasm mixed with ignorance?

The external view

Gregory (2017a) detailed the move away from subject survey inspections by Ofsted and highlighted other ways in which the current developments might be noted as well as how the opportunities for sustaining changes and improvements might be utilized. As the more formal constraints of external inspection and monitoring have lessened, there is now more scope for regulation and reflection by informed teachers of Art and Design themselves. These include a higher profile for subject leaders, active involvement in local and national networks as well as ongoing continuing professional development (CPD) in order to strengthen teachers' knowledge, understanding and skill base. We will return to this to consider how far it has become common practice in our schools.

Two years after the last Ofsted publication (Ofsted, 2012), a helpful guide was devised for non-specialist inspectors to use when making judgements about the effectiveness of the teaching of the subject during general inspections (Ofsted, 2014). Part of this guide is reproduced (see Figure 2.2) and it is worth noting it was designed to be a small aide memoire or prompt sheet inserted into a ring binder. The inspectors are reminded to look for exploratory activities with a wide range of media undertaken by the youngest pupils as a healthy foundation for developing ideas, experiences and imagination itself. This leads through 2D, 3D and digital media with older primary pupils towards mastery by learning about artists, makers and designers. The development of their knowledge around historic and cultural foundations can then be woven into a greater understanding of the subject and ensure the development of critical thinking. Inspectors are warned to look for more than repetitions of existing artworks, though with reminders about the importance of continued examples of pupil experimentation, invention and creation of their own and new work. To underline the importance of all this across the primary curriculum, Ofsted linked the activities to acts of creativity as the often 'messy' and unpredictable foundations for GCSE study at KS4. We would commend the guide (and the bullet point list of expectations included in Chapter 7) to any primary teacher wanting to ensure mastery in their school.

The importance of the impact of the above expectations becomes very clear when considered in the light of some other indicators of the current state of Art and Design. Firstly, the NSEAD survey (NSEAD, 2016) produced some shocking insights into the development of the subject in primary schools. The amount of time being allocated appeared to be reducing as teachers grappled with the increased pressure resulting

Figure 2.2 Ofsted expectations (2014)

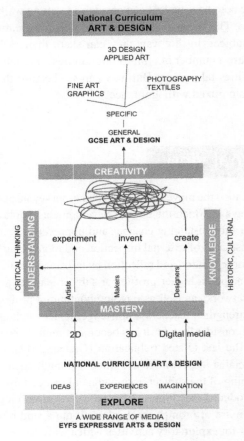

from the focus on literacy and numeracy. Teachers also reported that CPD opportunities were mirroring this, and that fewer chances were being made available to them to extend their knowledge of the subject. It also became clear that more teachers were self-funding courses and that more courses were being undertaken in the teachers' own time. Teachers entering the profession for the first time were also having considerably less training in Art and Design (Rogers, 2003; Corker, 2010; Gregory, 2017c) and many were struggling to utilize and apply experiences from their own childhood as a basis for teaching the subject. This does not seem to be a good starting point for contemplating the goal of mastery as outlined in this book, and it reinforces the need for teachers to be willing to engage with CPD – even to the point of organizing it for themselves. The increase in membership of NSEAD from teachers working in primary settings is itself a response to the low levels of provision from within the education system as a whole. (See Figures 2.3 and 2.4.)

Putting various sources together, we can start to illustrate the general position to be found in primary schools. There is likely to be a perceived hierarchy of subjects within the curriculum that regrettably positions Art and Design low on the list (DfEE, 1999;

Figures 2.3 and **2.4** CPD might mean teachers trying out their ideas

Herne, 2000) and the subjects 'valued' by external forces through national accountability measures at the top. The amount of time being devoted to the subject is diminishing (NSEAD, 2016). Schools may focus on certain art forms – for example, painting and drawing to the detriment of 3D forms and prefer 'clean' materials to 'messy' ones (Ofsted, 2012), and they may reinforce the work of certain artists – usually dead, male ones (Gregory, 2014). Most primary teachers have an insufficient experience and knowledge base from which to build their own confidence and teach the subject well, and they also tend to avoid contemporary art in their teaching (Eglington, 2003; Downing and Johnson, 2003; Ofsted, 2012). The subject is usually poorly resourced and too often led by a reluctant subject lead (Gregory, 2014), who may have little interest in it themselves. Opportunities for undertaking CPD are becoming very scarce and may require self-funding by the teachers wanting to utilize them (NSEAD, 2016).

Although this depressing picture might be a representation for many schools, it is not an accurate one in the schools that have understood the concept of mastery. In these, there is confident and inspirational leadership with clearly empowered champions for Art and Design (Ofsted, 2012; Gregory, 2014). The leadership of the subject involves many, including governors (NSEAD/Arts Council, 2016). Together they ensure a continual, reflective and effective review of the curriculum offered and make sure current female artists are both represented and celebrated. Similarly, large-scale work is evident around the school as are creatively used sketchbooks (March, 2016) by all pupils (and sometimes staff as well). Specific CPD is commissioned using galleries, universities and local artists and creative practitioners in order to strengthen and expand the confidence and understanding of the whole staff group (Strauss and Gregory, 2017). The main characteristic displayed in such vibrant school settings is one of embracing change and challenge with joy and creative application. They may engage in external events and activities organized by galleries or creative groups – including street festivals, competitions and exhibitions (Gregory and March, 2016). The making of art is viewed as cognitively demanding and teachers explore their learning contexts though action research or teacher enquiry (Blackmore and Crowe, 2016; Huxley, 2017).

A very different set of possibilities is clearly beginning to emerge and the reasons for this, together with the challenges and options for schools, will follow, as well as a discussion of the actions that individual teachers can take in order to make a difference.

Quick pause moment – *A scenario-based question*:

- NSEAD strongly supports teachers engaging with local networks of art teachers and having regular CPD.
- What CPD opportunities have you had in Art and Design in the past year (locally, regionally or nationally)?

The place of research in Art and Design education

In education, there is much mention these days of 'evidence-based' or 'research-led' practice (Nelson and O'Beirne, 2014). When it comes to teaching and learning in Art and Design the comparatively small pool of research evidence is all-too-often overlooked. Far too many teachers (and school leaders) remain woefully ignorant of the research into art education, the appropriate pedagogies and empowerment from art-making – either as a research base (especially for higher levels of study) or from active inclusion in a community of practice. We would therefore like to start with some explanation of the notion of research, and how it might be found, engaged with and applied into the active art class. (See Figure 2.5.)

Research is essentially about finding out and it can be undertaken at many different levels. Sometimes it is linked to formal qualifications or funded research projects but often it is undertaken by ordinary classroom teachers who just want to explore an aspect of learning in order to satisfy their own curiosity and improve their own practice. They may also be brave enough to share their investigations with others. Those who submit their work to a journal become actively engaged in disseminating their findings as much as those who attend conferences and speak directly to an audience. In the course of writing this book, we have tried to refer to a wide range of research and a variety of sources. It might be helpful to set out some of these sources for the reader's consideration.

Art and Design journals are usually associated with a particular academic community. Some have a particular geographic reach in mind (for example those published in Canada, the USA or Australia) others are intended for a wider audience and might be used as a provocation to investigate issues more deeply in one or more countries. There's a list of academic journals at the back of this book together with the details of the publishers, websites, etc. (see pp. 161–62). (For UK-based research we would recommend the *International Journal of Art and Design Education – iJADE*.) Journals are frequently used by student teachers in order to develop academic arguments

Figure 2.5 Working with made and found materials

in assignments but, sadly, then overlooked by them once they've qualified. The usual argument is that to access them a paid membership is required. This contrasts with the electronic databases that the university library service used at their training stage, which were perceived as free. In addition to subject association or organization membership, it is possible to extend membership of a university library and continue to use the journal search facility. It is also possible to combine both – as an individual or for a whole-school staff – through the Chartered College of Teaching (n.d.) and gain access to a similar database while also enjoying the benefits of a teacher-led network.

There are also refereed magazines published in most countries, but these may be more difficult to gain access to through the database system and membership of the publishing organization is required. Again, a list is provided at the end of this book (see pp. 159–60): the UK-based magazine is *AD magazine* published by NSEAD. (PDF versions of an earlier magazine called *StART* are available online to members of NSEAD, and the contents, projects and suggestions are still a rich and valid resource.)

In addition, some teacher-led communities have an online group, operate a website and encourage the sharing of ideas, support and resources. The weakest art-based resources online that we have found originate from individual teachers who do not have access to a critically supportive subject-based community. This is, unfortunately, the sharing of ignorance – something that we seek to avoid.

Drawing on this resource bank of research evidence, let's turn our attention to what we understand research in Art and Design education contributes to the development of the subject in the primary classroom.

What does the research actually say?

Pedagogy – This is a major consideration in developing Art and Design in the class-room. There are various forms that relate to the underlying theory of learning held by the teacher. A simple form was constructed (Gregory, 2006) after the basics of behaviourist and constructivist approaches in art teaching were identified by Little-dyke and Huxford (1998) and Hoye (1998). Table 2.1. sets out the main points where the forms could affect the way(s) in which attitudes, behaviours and expectations might all affect teaching and learning differently.

These provide a quick guide for teachers to consider the attitudes and behaviours that they hold themselves – or they perceive are held by their colleagues in the same school. It also points to some of the challenges they might want to bring in order to effect changes.

Addison and Burgess (2002) define in some detail what they refer to as 'the didactic/heuristic continuum' model (2002: 23) in which they specify five distinct forms of pedagogy utilized in Art and Design together with their impact on learning. They suggest that a very effective teacher of Art and Design can deliberately move between these forms according to the intended outcomes and demands of the learning process. In reality, over the past decade, our experience in observing primary teachers teaching the subject has been a reduction in their use and an over-reliance on the didactic/passive form. This isn't to say that the pupils do nothing but sit there while the teacher speaks (even though this may be more common that we suppose). In fact, the teacher often holds up the sole example of what should be achieved, and the pupils set about trying to make a copy.

Hallam, Das Gupta and Lee (2008) indicated that primary teachers often struggled to understand the demands of the curriculum and tended to compensate for this by over-relying on particular ways of teaching. As Addison and Burgess acknowledge there are positives and negatives (drawbacks) for each form of pedagogy (see Table 2.2, but it is regrettable that most primary teachers do not have the full range of the repertoire from which to select the most appropriate. Few research studies have explored the pedagogies of the art class in recent years but the reduction in awareness is less than surprising given the shortened time in which to learn during the teacher training experience (Gregory, 2017c). Teachers then can inadvertently reproduce their own experiences or limited understanding (Eglington, 2003).

Quick pause moment – *Thinking about what you currently do*:

- Where has your understanding of the pedagogies that you use actually come from?
- Either observe a colleague or ask a colleague (be brave) to record the number of forms of pedagogical styles you adopt in an Art and Design lesson.
- Reflect on the styles you thought you used and those you actually adopted. Any surprises?

Table 2.1 Key elements or characteristics of teachers of art

Key elements	Behaviourist	Constructivist
Teacher behaviour	Discourage learner interaction: the teacher 'provides' the information	Encourage learner interaction, student initiated questions and cooperative learning
Curriculum	Ignores or minimizes inter-curriculum links	Articulate the relevance of inter-curriculum links
Learner behaviour	Encourages learners to listen carefully and then undertake the exercises	Encourage learners to be responsible for their own learning
Feedback	May ignore practice activities – unless the product is flawed	Offer supportive feedback to learners while they are working
Artworks and process	Uses process to produce the product	Emphasize process rather than product
Organization for learning	Using the curriculum framework, provides learners with the appropriate categories to use	Focus on theme/elements, allowing learners to classify and organize subcategories for themselves
Attitude to new ideas	Criticizes products that do not replicate the template offered	Appreciate new and novel ideas/realities and value 'wonderment'
Attitude to new challenges	Value replication of artworks or techniques demonstrated; 'easy-step' approach may be used to achieve the desired outcome	Value curiosity, exploration, inquiry and 'risk and difficulty'
Attitude to created artworks	Appreciate consistent replication by pupils, not what they would like to create	Appreciate what pupils create, not what they can repeat
Attitude to problems	May view the learners as the problem – especially if their work is substandard	Pose challenging problems that relate to the learners
Value of artwork	Value each artwork according to the product criteria	Value each artwork if it is honestly created
Use of questions	Discourage questions generally, unless closed and reinforce the information already provided; clarity of teacher expectation increases certainty	Encourage open-ended questions and uncertainty

(Continued)

Table 2.1 (Continued)

Key elements	Behaviourist	Constructivist
Attitude to views of others	Only encouragement for pupils is to produce the desired outcome (empathy is not required)	Encourage pupils to see the views/ frames of others (empathy)
Attitude to wider perspectives	Encourage the adoption of single (implicitly correct) frames or perspectives	Encourage the adoption of multiple frames or perspectives
Underlying belief about teaching	Conviction that transmission is the best way to educate pupils	Consider transformation rather than transmission

Source: Gregory, 2006, after Littledyke and Huxford (1998) and Hoye (1998)

Table 2.2 Simplified didactic/heuristic continuum

Teaching forms	Learning forms
Didactic	Passive
Directed	Response and activity based
Negotiated	Active and experimental
Empowering/validating	Heuristic
Dependent/redundant	Open

Source: After Addison and Burgess, 2002

Curriculum and learning experiences – We are aware that the place of sculpture and 3D work is reducing in primary classrooms (Ofsted, 2012). This is often linked to time pressure on the curriculum and a need for reduction in messy activities but it may also be related to the knowledge and experience base that teachers draw upon. As we will explain later, the richness of learning through these forms and processes is something we hope that readers will restore in their classrooms. We know that children are not being taught to look and closely observe to the extent that they once were, again mainly due to the poorer experiential education of the teachers themselves, compounded by the reduction in time made available in their teacher training (Gregory, 2015). We also know that talking as a part of the making activities of Art and Design is crucial to the depth of the learning and the cognitive experience carried forward (Gregory, 2012). The importance, gender and role of the artists included in the curriculum can all be questioned in the light of the research above. Too many children may have heard about female or contemporary artists from outside of school, and yet, because of a lack of appreciation or knowledge on the part of their teachers, any discussions about 'role models' may not link to the artists actually studied (Freedman, 1994). Then there are a host of other issues affecting the learning experiences that haven't yet been fully investigated, for example: tidiness and the gendering of learning environments (Hopper, 2015), the blurring of Art and Design with Design Technology (Rutland, 2009), and the reduction in numbers of secondary schools offering non-English Baccalaureate subjects (Cultural Learning Alliance, 2014).

The list could be much longer, but let's turn to another aspect of research in the field of Art and Design.

Training teachers – The amount of time allocated to Art and Design in university-based initial teacher education (ITE) in the past twenty years has been greatly reduced (Rogers, 2003; Corker, 2010; Gregory, 2017c). In the last few years, the increase in school-based ITE has been noted, but, as yet, there are no details of the subject-specific contents or time allocations available. Anecdotally, there seems to be even less provision made, and the quality seems to reflect the concerns already noted (Eglington, 2003; Ofsted, 2009 2012). In short the training of future teachers is in flux and causing come apprehension for those concerned with the future of the subject.

New and developing threads – Controversy as a topic seems to be a strange inclusion here. Ofsted (2009) noted that such issues were often dealt with in school in Art and Design work. In view of this, it is worth considering the extent to which primary teachers already act as censors. Gregory (2014) highlighted how the decisions over which artworks were used in schools often hinged on the censorship activities of the teachers and, in particular, the subject leader. Referring to the infamous installation by Damien Hirst (*The Physical Impossibility of Death in the Mind of Someone Living*, 1991) several teachers explained that they couldn't show a photograph to their pupils as they could be frightened by the shark. Others denied access to works by Goya (as 'too gory') or Kahlo (as 'too dark'). The links between depth of subject knowledge, censorship and future experimentation are yet to be defined. Undoubtedly, they will be considered in parallel to the availability of training and the development of leadership, as we know these are required to redress the reluctance of primary teachers to embrace contemporary art (Adams et al., 2008).

Other projects that ought to be considered here include ways of giving greater autonomy to pupils. Room 13 (an international network of art studios in primary schools) does exactly that by allowing pupils to experience an art studio space in the school environment and make decisions over the appointment of artists-in-residence, as well as directing the project through their involvement in the management committee (Adams, 2005). Several galleries have also adopted a philosophical enquiry approach in order to develop greater engagement with artworks and build confidence (Strauss and Gregory, 2017). In this way, young people have become the leaders –

Figure 2.6 Room 13 offering studio opportunities

facilitating others as they deepen their appreciation or by defining the art developed in public spaces in their local area. Some schools have also taken the opportunity to use the Artsmark Award scheme as a means of driving development forward (Gregson, 2012). All of these examples empower pupils and have the potential to develop their learning far beyond the currently defined curriculum of most schools. (See Figure 2.6.)

New research opportunities?

As we have already noted, the excitement of fresh research areas is to be found by those willing to explore them. There are many such possibilities already waiting for courageous teachers to accept the challenge. Those who would aim to develop as masters in the subject must be aware that they could find themselves both leading innovative developments as well evaluating their impact by disseminating their research study to the wider community of Art and Design teachers, themselves eager to learn and apply this in their own classrooms.

We hope that this book will spur readers on to investigate their own research studies and in time also share this with us.

Quick pause moment – *Thinking about research*:

- What is there to stop you engaging in some structured action research of your own?
- Where would you turn to for support, encouragement and guidance?

How can teachers positively contribute to children's enjoyment of Art and Design?

The fuller answer is to be found throughout this book – especially in the coming chapters.

The summative version here is to ensure a number factors are addressed:

- Teachers need to prepare themselves – not being afraid to audit their experiences, knowledge and confidence and being prepared to extend and challenge themselves.

- Teachers can find their own enthusiasm and then be prepared to share it with their classes – while acknowledging that the learning process can be frustrating and difficult at times (thereby modelling the determination they'd like to develop in their pupils).

- Teachers can engage in new and creative training and development opportunities (even if it means challenging the current provision in school).

- Teachers can engage in active reflection about the teaching and learning they promote and experience.

- Teachers can celebrate successes, adventurous exploration and even developments that seem not to work.

- Teachers can critically analyse the planning process to ensure the best opportunities are provided, avoiding routes to orthodoxy and reinforcement of established norms.

- Teachers need to be knowledgeable, confident and able to be active and articulate advocates: they will not be restricted by the resources available or the environment.

- Teachers should inspire a willingness to explore new materials, techniques and opportunities (in their colleagues, teaching assistants and pupils).

- Teachers need to expose themselves to a broad range of art influences, galleries and artworks as well as finding ways of facilitating such opportunities for their pupils. (See Figures 2.7 and 2.8.)

Figures 2.7 and **2.8** Experimental teachers in action

The choices ahead

In 2014 a useful audit tool was published by the Art and Design Expert Subject Advisory Group (ESAG). This is included later in the book (see p. 000) as we think it can be of help to individual teachers or whole-school communities when considering how to identify and structure their actions to improve the teaching of Art and Design. A downloadable Word-based version is available from both ESAG and NSEAD websites.

Other forms of audit are available (see Bowden, Ogier and Gregory, 2013) to support the collection of information from members of staff. These can be invaluable tools in developing an understanding of a current baseline, working towards a defined action plan and ensuring targeted in-school CPD is appropriate.

Looking towards leadership in Art and Design education is an all-too-rare career trajectory. Understanding the basis of leadership and seizing the creative opportunities in order to affect children's, colleagues' and the wider community's understanding of the subject is crucial if mastery of Art and Design is to be fully achieved in the primary school. Those wanting to reflect on the overall quality of Art and Design provision made in their school may find the Ofsted grading process helpful as outlined in an earlier subject survey inspection report (Ofsted, 2009).

It would be exciting to encourage more research into Art and Design in the primary school. If readers would like to contact us (the authors), we would be happy to discuss further ways that this could be achieved and (if appropriate) linked to further study or qualifications.

Recommended reading

The following three texts are suggested as follow-on reading:

Gregory, P. (2012), 'Should Children be Learning to Make Art or Learning Through Art?' in M. Sangster (ed.), *Developing Teacher Expertise: Exploring Key Issues in Primary Practice*. London: Continuum.

Hallam, J., Das Gupta, M. and Lee, H. (2008), 'An Exploration of Primary School Teachers' Understanding of Art and the Place of Art in the Primary School Curriculum'. *Curriculum Journal*, 19(4), pp. 269–81.

Tutchell, S. (2014), *Young Children as Artists*. Abingdon: Routledge.

Chapter 3
Art and Design as an Irresistible Activity

This chapter will consider:

- What makes something irresistible?
- Why should Art and Design be full of irresistible activity?
- What does Art and Design look like as an irresistible activity?
- How can teachers make primary Art and Design irresistible?
- How can contemporary and modern art appreciation and critical awareness be included as an irresistible activity?

Quick pause moment

- Which words would you use to describe ***irresistible experiences***? See Figure 3.1.

Figure 3.1 Commonly used synonyms

These richly persuasive words have the capacity to lure and engage willing participants to 'have a go' and be involved in an experience. In whatever form that may take, these words are generic to irresistible encounters, whether an ice-cold glass of water on a very hot day, untrodden snow, the smell of a strong cup of coffee first thing in the morning or a particularly inviting window of a shop. These feelings are innate to the human psyche, though undeniably subjective – what is irresistible to one person, is often entirely different to another.

Importantly, it is the emotional and inspirational aspect of the irresistible urge that we will focus on in this chapter, in order to understand and ensure that we utilize it within our teaching and learning of Art and Design.

What makes something irresistible?

The precise moment of fascination that hooks the learner and thus the experience posed to them is the very essence of a rich learning encounter. In his article about affect and art in the classroom, Addison (2011) refers to these irresistible moments as 'intensities' where the learner is affected so deeply by the learning experience that they become intensely involved both mentally and physically in that moment.

> Affect produces attention that brings its trigger into consciousness.
>
> (Addison, 2011: 365)

During these moments of extreme consciousness, sensory awareness is heightened and we, as human beings, are engaged with both body and mind. There is no defined time attached but these moments are richly sensorial and experiential in their nature. If we allow it, they have the power to slow us down, take stock, enjoy and indulge in a moment of intense engagement. We can relate this to any learning experience; it may be completely new to us or based on something we already know. Whatever the premise, they are experiences that provoke a reaction and release an urge to engage.

> A painting is a record of the extremely intensified moments of life – where more than one space, two senses of time, more than the law even seems at work, where the emotional forces seem to be propelling one to a dangerous limit, where reason and explanations become too enfeebled or too speeded-up to matter.
>
> (Brett Whiteley, artist, 1967)

It would be pertinent and highly relevant within the technoculture of today to momentarily consider the negative side of irresistible in relation to what twenty-first-century children consider to be tantalizing. It could be argued that, to a primary school-aged child, age-old experiences are still highly tempting – such as baking a cake, creating a model with clay, opening a new set of felt-tips, kicking a gleaming new football or walking across a frosty field of grass. This list, thankfully, is still endless. However, intentionally not included here are 'screen-related' activities. The irresistible urge to pick up a laptop, iPad, Xbox, etc. has become a current reality for all young children and, in truth, is an overwhelming desire for many that can often override the previously mentioned tactile and visual experiences. On-screen activity is a reality of today, and one that needs careful consideration, in order to maximize its creative potential and minimize the risks and dangers.

> And as the technological landscape changes, childhood and youth, too, transform. Children and young people are increasingly connected around the clock, and have

a parallel existence in virtual space, seamlessly integrated with their actual lives. They are skilful collaborators, capable of knowledge-making as well as information-seeking. They engage in social networks, they navigate digital gaming and they generate and manipulate digital content. They experiment in new ways with forms of their own social face.

(Craft, 2012: 2)

It would be hard to deny that a lot of screen-based activity is sedentary and that this existence lures children from the youngest of ages. In order to fully engage with this twenty-first-century child, we must recognize that this is the world they have grown up in and live in, but, at the same time, we can and should offer some alternatives. If we tap into the ingredients that make an alternative experience just as irresistible as that of the iPad, etc., we will contemporaneously hook young minds and ensure the enthralling emotions of the screen will be equally realized with our active activities and experiences – if not bettered!

The ever-growing domain of screen-based engagement, and the arguments for and against, are immensely controversial subjects. For the purposes of our discussion, we need to consider at this juncture what it is that makes this digital world so irresistible to our children. We can then utilize this knowledge to inform our plans on how to engage these children in other forms of experience that are just as alluring but also, and very importantly, exercise both body and mind in a more physically and sensory-based moment. Children's ability to luxuriate in a sensory-driven moment, as they excel in the delights of that experience and all it offers, is commensurate with their twenty-first-century aptitudes and attitudes to learning and erudition. When observing children and young people's interactions with digital-based devices, it is easy to see that the visual, lightweight, portable and highly intuitive characteristics are very appealing and respond to a tactile and haptic sense of engagement (Merchant, 2015). Merchant (2012) refer to this contemporary technological relationship as 'the allure of the new and "shiny"'.

The powerful surges of excitement that such an experience can provoke are absolutely what moments in Art and Design should be about, as they have the power to draw in and arrest, be it for the purpose of enlightenment or pleasure of surprise (Addison, 2011). We, therefore, need to consider how to take these qualities of willing engagement in order to contextualize and physicalize them within Art and Design learning.

Why should Art and Design be full of irresistible activity?

Irresistible art experiences entice the viewer, spectator, participator to become intrigued and involved and so become absorbed into an experience that conjoins curiosity, creativity and excitement. This experiential process is as much to do with the act of looking at and experiencing the art produced by others as it is being the artist themselves. We need to consider how to entice and intrigue our children, and fellow teachers, to such an extent that they cannot resist the art activity, materials and opportunities on offer in order for them to fully experience the wonders and possibilities of art.

If we make our art teaching and learning irresistible, then it should follow that the participants simply cannot help themselves but be curious, become motivated and get involved. This sequence is powerful; the teacher has successfully engaged the children, they are keen and willing and therefore will become immersed in the learning experience. All credit due to that initial irresistibility.

Let us consider now how this would work with our current primary education system. Schools and, as a consequence, children, live in a SATs-driven and core subject-led educational climate, which often looks to the next stage rather than living and existing in the here-and-now. In 2000, with the introduction of numeracy and literacy strategies, Herne noted that most art at primary schools was being taught in the afternoon and, owing to few opportunities for art-based training, teachers were becoming deskilled. A shared vision for art as an important subject was gradually dwindling (Herne, 2000). In 2009, nine years on from these somewhat depressing observations, the Cambridge Primary Review (2010) warned that teaching to the test in primary schools had become endemic, sapping the enthusiasm of teachers and pupils alike. So now here we are in 2018 and both these statements continue to ring true.

All too often, an art session within a primary classroom is the result of a humanities-based theme, and it is used to illustrate a written story or is included in 'golden time'. It most likely takes place in an afternoon, generally on a Friday. This scenario rarely allows for the session to be wholeheartedly offered as a learning opportunity to immerse oneself in. As time is limited, the potential values of art are diminished. What is often missing is the 'hook' that entices the participant, the element that stimulates, the ingredient that makes this learning moment utterly irresistible. That hook is the essence of a lesson start-up and it is crucial to get this right and ensure it is at the heart of the initial planning process. If the children are hooked, they are far more likely to learn.

> As teachers, it's our job to ensure that the flame of learning gets kindled and burns brightly for all, whatever their capacity, interests or age. But we need to think really carefully about what we put children through, because there's no way we can engage them through more years of study if they've already run out of appetite.
>
> (The Guardian, 'The Secret Teacher', 16 May 2015)

A powerful lesson, more often than not, has its roots in a highly irresistible initial stimulus that hooks the children from the outset (Bloomfield and Childs, 2013).

On the more positive side there are plenty of schools still championing art and producing some phenomenally creative work. With the ongoing support and lobbying of organizations such as NSEAD, art teaching professionals continue to fly the flag of what is irresistible and essential about Art and Design within the primary curriculum.

> NSEAD believes that a world class art, craft and design education provides and inspires personal expression, personal understanding, creative and practical

responses, promoting imaginative risk taking to provide solutions to our material, emotional, social and virtual worlds.

(NSEAD, 2014: 3)

There is no doubt that there is overwhelming pressure in our British education system for the school community to work towards results, with data and pupil progress based on continual, never-ending assessment. This is not to say that assessing our children is not important – of course it is essential, so that we can differentiate and plan for them appropriately. However, it seems that only a small percentage of that knowing and planning relates wholeheartedly to them, their characters, their idiosyncrasies and their sensitivities (Eglinton, 2003) Children are emotional and expressive beings, who do seem to spend a lot of their time in this current climate, sitting at desks and being assessed. Teachers also suffer from this regime as they preplan their days, worrying about timings, pace, expectation of data and the pressure of the top-down approach. Most worryingly, there is a heavy reliance on assessment data, tests and highly prescriptive timetables. Such an existence is echoed by a primary school teacher when she laments

We find ourselves forcing a curriculum solely dominated by literacy and numeracy, measurable by tests, on children, which destroys their interest in learning.

(Sarah Marsh, *The Guardian*, 5 July 2017)

Quick pause moment *What happens in your class?*

- How often do the children in your class have opportunities for art-making each week?
- Do you offer art activities that can be returned to and continued as an ongoing, developing project?
- Over the past term, when has art taken place in your classroom – in an afternoon, during an art week, once in the term?

If we have a look at an example of a spring term timetable for a Year 4 class (Table 3.1) the schedule is clearly dominated by core subject sessions. A mere 30 minutes is dedicated to Art and Design on a Friday afternoon.

Such short periods of learning and teaching in art leaves very few intervals for moments of intense irresistible learning where young minds have the space and time to think, express and animate their ideas and utilize their imaginations and artistic endeavours. Included in this lament of time restrictions is the worry that less time is given to emotive and provocative learning scenarios that successfully explore and encourage children to think and feel emotionally about topics, subjects and situations. As they are hurried through their curriculum timetables with every hour and minute being accounted for, they can afford little time to really think and feel. They

Table 3.1 Example Year 4 timetable

Time	Monday	Tuesday	Wednesday	Thursday	Friday
8.55 a.m.	Registration	Registration	Registration	Registration	Registration
9.10 a.m.–9.30 a.m.	Whole-school assembly	Maths	Maths	Whole-school assembly	Whole-school assembly
9.30 a.m.–10.00 a.m.	Maths	10.10 a.m. KS2 assembly		Maths	Maths
10.30 a.m.–10.45 a.m.	Break	Break	Break	Break	Break
11.10 a.m.–12.10 p.m.	Literacy	Literacy	Literacy	Literacy	Literacy
12.10 pm–1.00 p.m.	Lunch	Lunch	Lunch	Lunch	Lunch
1.00 p.m.–1.30 p.m.	Guided reading	Science	Guided reading	Guided reading	Guided reading
	French		Library	ICT	**Art**
2.00 p.m.–3.00 p.m.	Topic		PE	RE	PHSE

need this valuable time in order to grow and flourish as highly ordered, thinking young beings, As Eglinton so rightly points out:

> A child's inner world is so spectacularly huge it could literally stimulate and motivate years and years of art experiences.
>
> (Eglington, 2003: 29)

So a further consideration as to why art should be irresistible is rooted in the allowance and recognition it makes for individual expression, sensitive responses and personal interpretation. These reactions require the child to dig deep and make contact with their essential emotions, which help them understand the world around and help them to live effectively (Claxton, 2006).

What does Art and Design look like as irresistible activity?

> Art is the only way to run away without leaving home.
>
> (Twyla Tharp, 2008)

What makes art such a powerful medium and subject for exciting learning is its capacity to entice and motivate the learner. This is a subject that has the capacity to provoke and amaze the viewer, participant and emerging artist if the experience is full and wonderful in its existence.

Figure 3.2 presents views of what art looks like as an irresistible activity according to: teacher training students, children and a practising artist:

Figure 3.2 Some views on art as an irresistible activity

Y2 BA ED students:

'Getting lost in it and forgetting about your worries'

'Expressing yourself without using words'

'Watching your work grow'

'It's very personal'

Year 6 child:

'Art is loads of things and you can express yourself in whatever you do – you are FREE!' Year 3 child:

Fiona Rae, artist:

"What I love about painting is that it embodies a series of thought and feeling processes. It's all there on the canvas as a record. I can put something on the canvas, consider it, adjust it, remove it, replace it, add to it, conceal it, reveal it, destroy it and repair it. I can be in a good mood, a bad mood, a cheerful mood or a destructive mood - it's all useful."
- Fiona Rae (Fiona RaeSunday 20 September 2009 The Observer)

So, how do we link such inspirational art practice to art in the primary classroom? What does it mean for our children and the primary curriculum? What does it mean for our teachers and art in the primary curriculum? Most importantly, how can we ensure that it does exist, and that it happens on a regular, necessary basis?

How can teachers make primary Art and Design irresistible?

The number of motivational ideas is endless. Inside the minutes of any chosen hour inspirational opportunities continuously present themselves; whether we grab hold of these opportunities depends upon our ability to recognise them. ... We will never be short of ideas to ignite and perpetuate the artistic experiences.

(Eglington, 2003: 34)

To make Art and Design irresistible the teacher must commit to providing opportunities that incite feelings of surprise and, thus motivational discovery and learning. This teaching approach is exciting – it allows the practitioner to consider what is tempting in learning, what drives an individual to find out and discover. The teacher needs to remember what it is about learning that makes it irresistible, and then design their lessons, their spaces of learning and their teaching materials accordingly. This is not teaching that rigidly conforms to an instructional, target-bound paradigm. It is essential to provide classrooms that have no ceiling when creative minds are operating and finding out. Classrooms of young children should be alive and 'scandalous' (Giudici and Vecchi, 2004). As Eisner (2002) reflects:

When there is no challenge, when everything is satisfactory, there may be little motivation to stretch one's thinking, to try something new, to experiment, to revise, to appraise, and to start again.

(Eisner, 2002: 36)

Irresistible art should be dynamic and changeable, encouraged by a theme of the moment or an interest that pervades children's imaginations and takes them to alternative spheres of thinking. Claxton (2006) refers to these as 'wild topics' and insists that their installation encourages and strengthens a space that challenges and extends the learner.

The key aspects of 'wild topics' or themes:

● Rich – there is much to be explored

● Challenging – the topic contains real difficulty

● Extended – there is time and opportunity to go into it in depth

● Relevant – the topic connects with children's own interests and concerns

● Responsibility – children have some genuine control over what, why, how and when they organize their learning

- Real – solving the problem or making progress genuinely matters to someone
- Unknown – the practitioner does not already know the 'answer'
- Collaborative – most children enjoy the opportunity to work together with others on such tasks'

(Tutchell, 2014: 138)

Characteristic of this irresistible pedagogical approach is a commitment to heuristic and affective teaching (Addison, 2011). Although there are plans in place, the outline is not prescriptive, and the outcome is open to interpretation. So it follows that individual and personal creativity is alive and kicking.

The following two case studies offer scenarios where irresistible learning was at the heart of Art and Design experience for both the educators and the learners.

CASE STUDY

1. **Playful provocations**: a collaborative dialogue through drawing

A group of trainee teacher students, who were also art specialists in the first year of their degree, collaboratively designed a variety of art activities with the intention of provoking and enticing their non-art tutors and lecturers into actively participating as willing artists. The project coincided with the Big Draw (an arts education charity, which launches a drawing-related theme to encourage a nationwide celebration of drawing every October) and so was designed as a stimulus that would encourage everyone to want to draw, colour, design and create irrespective of their past and present woes and worries associated with talents and abilities in art.

> By fostering a greater understanding of what drawing can mean, and by increasing awareness and engagement, we believe many more people can benefit from, and contribute to society by drawing.
>
> (Big Draw website, 2016)

The students had been considering the reticence and fear that they often witness in the KS2 classroom from children who sensed an unwelcome challenge and had a 'fear of failure' attitude when entering into an art activity. By emulating this within a safe 'adult-based' environment, they were interested to see how easy or difficult it would be to provoke and intrigue the fearful adult who could be heard to say the words 'I can't draw', as so often heard within a KS2 classroom. As an aside, the students had also been discussing the plateau experienced at eight, nine or ten years old, when art-making is less prolific and purposeful, representational images dominate expectation.

They intentionally considered the word 'provoke' in their planning discussions in its definition as a promise of excitement and reaction (*Oxford Dictionary Online*, 2016). This powerful emotive response was their goal, in order to ensure that, whatever they designed as an activity, it would be irresistible to the beholder.

They considered the words of Adams (2016) in order to make meaning of the drawing activities they would proceed to entice their tutors with – they were constructing a weekly 'communication' dynamic through image-making;

Drawing as communication is that which assists the process of making ideas, thoughts and feelings available to others. Here, the intention is to communicate sensations, feelings or ideas to someone else.

(Adams, 2016: 163)

Quick pause moment:

Can you identify the hallmarks of irresistible learning? (The next section should help.)

What was irresistible?

Accessible and achievable

Their activities were simple and highly accessible responding to the process of sensory investigation: haptic and visual as well as ensuring a sense of success and pride in the end product. The students had to consider the non-art tutor 'character' – what would move and ignite the imaginations of this older and slightly reticent generation.

It takes imagination on the part of the young people to perceive openings through which they can move.

(Greene, 1995: 14)

To draw absent-mindedly and scrawl aimlessly were two historical definitions of 'doodle'. Both these appealed to the students as doodling is something most people do – often without intention but usually with ease. It felt accessible. Nothing concrete needed to come out of a doodle except the doodle itself, whether it showed an obvious representation in its final image or whether it actually represented the thoughts and emotions present while the action takes place. As said, importantly, it is something everyone does. So 'doodle' became a starting point. This was then partnered with sentiments from the Big Draw website:

When we draw, we take an opportunity to slow down, and to appreciate how the visual world works. By developing this skill we gain a deeper understanding of our surroundings and learn a truly universal language. A drawing can communicate an idea more effectively than words.

(Big Draw, 2016)

Below are three of the student-designed irresistible activities:

Wire-a-doodle:

Bend and twist your wire to represent your week so far. This is a simple activity that avoided the 'but I can't draw' response from participants. (See Figure 3.3.)

Hair-a-doodle:

'Give the dude a hairstyle.' By preparing a sheet with cut-out images of famous people's faces, the audience was drawn into adding a hairstyle that may have totally altered the original face – rendering even the most famous celebratory unrecognizable. (See Figure 3.4.)

Doodle-a-bauble:

Create your own wax-relief bauble so that it begins to look a lot like Christmas!' This activity could easily be adapted for other times in the year, but just look at the seasonal responses recorded in Figure 3.5.

As the activities rolled out, some very interesting observations were made in relation to the involvement and willingness of the vast majority of tutors (20 out

Figure 3.3 Wire-a-doodle

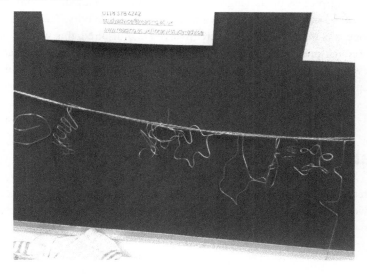

Figure 3.4 Hair-a-doodle

of a possible 26). The students were delighted with this number, particularly since these teaching professionals taught a range of subjects, including maths, science, English, and so were participating in a non-core subject activity. The students' overriding hope was that, if the tutors were involved and inspired, this would encourage them to rethink previous negative thoughts in relation to their own art-making and skills development. These positive encounters could then, in turn, influence their subject specialist students who had, at times, been in the habit of undermining art as a subject.

Collaborative engagement

The patterns of engagement in Figure 3.6 were commensurate with the tutors' emotional involvement in all the activities offered over the three months of investigation.

Figure 3.5 Doodle-a-bauble

Figure 3.6 Patterns of collaborative engagement

Patterns of Collaborative Engagement:

• Social engagement: dialogue, disclosing, laughter
• Peer encouragement: fun, collaboration, creativity, revealing
• Continuation: linking ideas, bonding, tangents, directions
• Process: ongoing, adventurous, experimental, unexpected
• Expanding repertoire: skills, ideas, possibilities

Tutchell and Vinney (2016)

CASE STUDY

2. **The Magic eggs of the Nile crocodiles:** Year 4

A treasured legacy from the pre-2014 National Curriculum was the inclusion of interesting and inspiring historical and geographical topics such as the Tudors, the Second World War and the Mayans. This particular Year 4 class were deeply ensconced in studying the Ancient Egyptians. As part of their homework, they had enthusiastically and imaginatively made pyramid sculptures, using a variety of sculptural materials ranging from Lego, cardboard and Weetabix to sugar. Following on from this, and ensuring a realization of what had hooked them to be imaginative for this 3D task, the lesson planned linked to sculptural work and the mystical aspects of the Ancient Egyptians as something that had really captured the children's imagination within this premise.

A story was told to the children about how, back in the times of the Pharaohs and Pyramids, there lived a float of very special crocodiles. These crocodilian reptiles were particularly unusual because once every ten years, when there was a full moon in the night sky, they would lay magic eggs. Under the magnificent glow of the full moon, the eggs would glint and sparkle, lighting up the riverbeds like beautiful fairy lights …

This is how the story began. The children, following the art lesson, would continue to write this story, spurred on by their imaginative 'making' of the magic eggs.

Each child was given an orange-sized ball of clay to sculpt into a hollow oval shaped egg, left open at the bottom in order insert a tea light.

Quick pause moment:

Can you identify the hallmarks of irresistible learning? (The next section should help.)

What was irresistible?

Let's consider a number of issues in turn.

Context and meaning

The children were already intrigued by the history-based topic, the mysterious structures and the stories of pharaohs, mummies, burials and sphynxes. Therefore, the magic egg of the Nile was in keeping with their interests and developing knowledge – it meant something to them, and it was meaningful and related to learning and understanding that they had previously encountered (Malin, 2013). It was also linked to the sculptural homework projects, so their involvement with manipulating and shaping materials was current and in their minds. For both these reasons, the eggs were contextual and meaningful for the children and so they were genuinely intrigued and motivated.

The initial hook and capture

As the children entered the class after a busy lunchtime, a previously made clay egg was alight on a central table. The visual wonderment caught them off guard and the questions started – 'What's that?', 'Why's it in here?', 'Who brought it in?'.

Intentionally, there were no answers given until all were seated around the egg and ready for the story. The story was told through the children eliciting ideas so that they were very much a part of why it existed – adding little extras and therefore owning the story as it developed. They were hooked by the visual enticement and the collaborative storytelling.

The classroom and design of space

An additional hook that had caught their attention, was the setup of the classroom. As opposed to the usual fairly sedentary setup there were no chairs, only tables and, on each table, lay a lump of clay.

> Creative episodes exist in the culture of the environment; a culture that opens up possibilities and critical thinking that is at the heart of our spaces.
>
> (Tutchell, 2014: 121)

The clay

The brown, sticky-looking substance was highly inviting. As the children began to play with the clay, they experienced its tactile properties; the soft, manipulative, malleable, mouldable and expressive qualities. They experienced a sensory 'awakeness' (House, 2011) in response to the earthy smell and agglutinative touch as they worked the clay. Their hands were covered with a brown silt that both amused and delighted them. The sculptural process was overwhelmingly irresistible in its sensory splendour and they were hooked. (See Figures 3.7, 3.8 and 3.9.) Prentice aptly describes this wonderful moment of playful yet purposeful handling of a tactile material such as clay:

> Handled in such a playful way, objects cease to be context-bound, and we can change their colour, texture, scale and function. Objects can stand for anything we choose; they become visual metaphors invested with personal meanings which suit our present purpose.
>
> (Prentice, 1995: 128)

Time and space for trial and error

In this Year 4 class, art was usually awarded a 30-minute slot on a Friday. On this occasion, the teacher (who incidentally was a newly qualified teacher (NQT) and was conscious of school rules and expectations) had become, in response to the material and the children's excitement, highly involved. She was therefore able to ignore the rigidity of time and opened up the entire afternoon to continued art heaven. A longer session ensured that time and space were positively utilized. The children were able to:

Figures 3.7, 3.8 and 3.9 Illustrations of the irresistibility of working with clay

- experiment and explore the material before they started the process of making their egg;
- understand the process of trial and error;
- review and revisit;
- celebrate and critique the end products as a collaborative group.

In contact with the children's hands, the malleable material underwent many transformations (Vecchi and Giudici, 2004). These gestures and forms belonged to the children, which they mentally catalogued as they continued to try out shapes, lines and forms.

The teacher's own engagement

> The child and teacher are thought of as colleagues searching, exploring, flowing with, and at the same time, guiding the experience.
>
> (Tutchell, 2014: 26)

There is no doubt that a pivotal aspect of what made this particular afternoon's art experience irresistible was the visible interest emanating from the class teacher. She was just as keen as the children to work with the clay and experience its qualities. Her own heightened creative and imaginative responses were consequently played out in the children and so their co-exploration confirmed a lively and inspired partnership in the learning scenario. It was interesting to discover that this was the first time she had worked with clay herself since a young child.

The role of the adult

Riding the wave (Tutchell, 2014) with the children, encourages both the child and the adult to engage in a respected union of interest – their responses to the art-making can be discussed, considered and employed but all within a constructively mutual and trusting platform from which to learn. The importance of creating relationships and shared moments that engage trust, autonomy and stimulation are vital elements of positive adult engagement. They make an irresistible moment a valued and recognized ingredient in a day of teaching.

The shared physical exploration produces shared moments of tactile and visual discoveries. A joint journey between child and adult gives rise to a growing sense of self-esteem in the child, as their adventure is being valued by someone else, and someone who, with careful and considered language, can extend the journey to a higher level of thinking. Children are more than capable of higher levels of thinking. So when working alongside a reflective and responsive adult, the 'thinking in art' moment is given an opportunity to expand and reveal further layers of understanding.

> Manipulating art materials integrates sensorimotor skills and other forms of reasoning, feeling and learning to emerge, … a somatic knowing – exchanges between the psyche (mind) and the soma (body).
>
> (Wright, 2010: 170)

Quick pause moment – *Thinking more about your experience*:

- When was the last time you invested time into a co-explore art activity with a child/children?
- How do you effectively talk to the children you teach about their artwork during and on completion of a project?
- Are there particular materials that invoke a collaborative teacher/child engagement?

Hooks and roots

As revealed in the second case study, an irresistible hook is essential. It gathers the children in, and it slows them down so that they can concentrate on the 'art' of the lesson about to follow. It is crucial in order to gain their attention and motivate them. There is currently a tendency, at the beginning of any lesson, to herd children in, wait for them to be seated and ready, ask them to write down the date and the learning objective then be ready with their whiteboards to begin a lesson. This may well ensure discipline and the collective quiet of thirty uniformed children, but it is unlikely to engage their creative young minds in order to motivate and inspire towards learning. This does not mean to say teaching needs to always be 'all singing' and 'all dancing' with dynamic hooks. But there is certainly a need not to be ruled by the writing of learning objectives before the children have even had a chance to be a part of the learning and understand what it is they are writing in their books. A hooked and irresistible experience should start them off and *then* the learning objectives can be *elicited* from the children. For one primary school the purposeful and meaningful hook is at the top of the certainties list when considering their lesson plans:

> Purpose: Learning should be rooted in real-life situations, which will hook the children and engage them throughout the lesson.
>
> (Oxford Road Community School, 2016)

An important aspect of lesson planning is both the awareness of and the response to what was previously learned. This ensures a meaningful link for the children and continues to build on what they already know. Importantly it guarantees that what is being planned relates to them and their interests, their learning behaviours and their roots. Their creative work in art is rooted in their personal experience and existence. These roots give them the confidence to venture forth and continue their foraging in the world of art-based learning. Advancement of knowledge grows from an established root of understanding. It is a bedrock seed that is deeply embedded in the child's cognitive and physical being and is integral to their artistic development.

The rooted 'seed' of experience, rich in creative knowledge, encourages children to use their art/play experiences as firm foundations for understanding themselves as artists. Cox (2005) refers to this work in progress along with continued enquiry as a young child's 'central source of data'. In reference to our second case study, the children knew that by soaking the clay with more and more water, they could squidge and squeeze the sticky mass, letting it slide between their fingers and creating weird and wonderful landscapes. They only knew this because they were given time to play with the clay before creating an end product. This process laid firm foundations of knowledge about how the material could be moulded and managed.

In our example of clay manipulation, the process was explored through playing with possibilities; the children utilized their idiosyncratic tendencies to subvert 'reality' and, in effect, create new realities (Cox, 2005). The layering of idiosyncratic ideas as well as newly found knowledge built the children's confidence as sculptural artists. Their discoveries were a part of the intricate web of growing sensory awareness that was unique to them. As they played, they developed their skill and understanding of how to use and be discerning with their senses.

Not only should we consider the roots of played experience, but also the children themselves – who they are and what makes them individuals. It would be impossible to ensure an irresistible hook that relates to thirty individuals on every occasion, but it is not impossible to consider hooks that call upon events, cultural backgrounds, family occasions, weekend experiences, etc.

> Art making always occurs in a cultural context, and so understanding who children are as artists requires looking at how they situate their art making in their cultural setting.
>
> (Malin, 2013: 8)

A hook that relates to something familiar can often be just as enticing and irresistible as one that relates to an unknown. In fact for some children the latter can be very daunting. Previous learning and building on the familiar does need recognition in order to tempt some of our children into having a go and getting involved. Children's explorations are rooted in what they already know – they build on the familiar to discover the unfamiliar.

> Unfamiliar experiences will spark and ignite the imagination and then connections will be traced back to an existing known.
>
> (Tutchell, 2014: 128)

How can contemporary and modern art appreciation and critical awareness be included in irresistible activity?

Challenges and taking risks, contemporary art and galleries

Within the realms of the unfamiliar, we can encourage children to take risks and challenge the norm. This does not mean to say that we always present them with hurdles to jump over and difficult goals to reach. But it does mean that we should offer opportunities that challenge their thinking and give rise to a confidence in risk-taking. This emotional state is critical to children's ability to think for themselves, push themselves further and experiment with new concepts and ideas. Unless we attempt to tantalize their thinking and involvement, we will be doing them a disservice and, importantly, restrict a higher order of thinking that is crucial to their developing minds and ability to synthesize and analyse knowledge (Roland, 2001).

Risk-taking and challenge in Art and Design can take a variety of forms. It may be that the irresistible hook is a new and enthralling sculptural material that has not been previously encountered. It may be an example of contemporary artwork being introduced for perusal and discussion. It may be a trip to a gallery to see a thought-provoking exhibition. All these experience give rise to that feeling of the 'five Ws and an H' – what, why, when, who, where, how – all essential dialogic and motivational enquiries when our human minds have been jolted into wanting to know because the root of the enquiry was irresistible . We could call all of these contemporary practices. A practice that is based in the here-and-now and considers new ways of looking, doing and creating. It is a practice within the contemporary classroom that requires the children to engage with artworks and art-making in new and different ways (Page et al., 2006).

What is important is that, in order to tempt and involve our primary-school-aged children in deep thinking and learning within Art and Design, we must allow them the pleasure of working with what is contemporary and not always resort to the safe art of yesterday. As contemporary twenty-first-century children, as previously discussed, they must be allowed the opportunity to see what art is being produced now as well as in the past so that they can continue to develop new ways of thinking, seeing and understanding and so become our new generation of contemporary artists.

> The underlying social critique and interrogation of identity associated with contemporary art practices, when employed within contexts of learning and teaching introduces a radical view of our understanding of the learner, the teacher, the process and the product.
>
> (Page et al., 2006: 154)

In conjunction with contemporary art in the classroom, it is also important to emphasize here that this should include art that is culturally and politically aware and without gender bias. Our children have the potential to grow up in a wonderfully global world where intercultural awareness is part of their everyday lives. What is essential is that they are exposed to a whole variety of richly diverse aspects of the world they live in so that they grow up with a true and meaningful understanding of global citizenship and gender equality (Chambers, 2014). This is where art plays such an important role, as it enables children and young people to contribute as confident citizens and future professionals to the culture, creativity, economic success, leisure and material and emotional well-being of our society within both national and global contexts (Gast, 2014).

When introducing children to contemporary artwork of the twentieth and twenty-first century, there is no doubt that you provoke reactions and sensibilities. This will, in turn, incite discussion, analysis, opinion and ongoing thinking, sometimes about tricky issues (Ogier, 2017). A few good and meaty examples of contemporary art, within the context of the lesson being taught, will entice the learner to an open-ended dialogue owing to the need to voice their opinion – another example of irresistible art.

Quite often, it is the more unusual artworks that trigger awareness (Addison, 2011).

Using art to explore cultural and social issues links contextual and critical study in the classroom to global citizenship and a developing awareness of the diverse range of artists around the world. Not only can this often represent multifarious classrooms but also brings in an understanding of a variety of cultural and indigenous aspects of the increasingly intercultural world that children of today live in. Contemporary art produced by both women and men is also vital in our promotion and reflection of a gender equal society as opposed to the too-often studied white male artists of the nineteenth century. The irresistible aspect of looking, analysing and debating will then become far more prevalent and recognized as an essential part of Art and Design in the primary classroom. The following two activities actively encourage and inspire such critical thinking and offer opportunities for irresistible, active and lively discussions using art and visual/tactile perceptions as a learning tool.

Last space in the gallery

One last space is left in the gallery for an artwork to be installed. Choose one piece of artwork from the examples below that you think deserves the space and one that you would never select. (More often than not, it is the latter that causes more animated discussion – what the participants do *not* like.) The selection made can only be agreed if the curator (who chooses the artwork) can give reasons relating to critical appreciation and reasoning. The selection has been intentionally chosen to represent forms of abstract and representational art over the period of the last 150 years in order to provoke discussion and response to the extremes of two-dimensional art:

- Berthe Morisot, *Summer's Day*, 1879
- Paul Cézanne, *Card Players*, 1895
- Joan Miro, *Catalan Landscape*, 1924
- Paul Klee, *Fire Evening*, 1929
- Sonia Delauney, *Rhythm*, 1938
- Mark Rothko, *No. 13*, 1940
- Helen Frankenthaler, *Canyon*, 1965
- Georg Baselitz, *Adieu*, 1982
- Bridget Riley, *Nataraja*, 1993
- Julie Mehretu, *Excerpt (Suprematist Evasion)*, 2003
- Ibrahim el-Salahi, *Tree*, 2003
- Tomma Abts, *Tys*, 2010
- Fiona Rae, *The Sun Throws My Sorrow Away*, 2012
- Rafa Forteza, *Espera Sosegada II 2014*

Art in public, or perhaps in surprising places, might also draw our curiosity …

The Fourth Plinth

Located in Trafalgar Square, the Fourth Plinth was built in 1841 and was intended to hold a statue of William IV, but, due to insufficient funds, it remained empty. Over 150 years later, the Fourth Plinth now hosts a series of commissioned artworks by world-class artists and is the most talked about contemporary art prize in the UK.

From the selection of classical and contemporary artworks offered to you what would you choose for the next Fourth Plinth artwork and why?

In your decision-making, think about the sculptural and haptic qualities and elements that might guide your choice:

Mass	Weight
Space	in between or around
Plane	length and width
Line	all that is visible
Movement	position and structure
Texture	tactile and haptic
Colour	natural or man-made
Relief	in the round or a specific viewing point
Scale	Dimension
Purpose	because or just is
Site	place and location

Figure 3.10 Laura Ford, *Rag and Bone*, 2007

Ford's socially and politically charged figures are human in scale or slightly larger than life-sized and exist somewhere between the realms of fantasy and reality, childhood and adulthood. *Rag and Bone* was based on the Beatrix Potter character, Mrs Tiggywinkle and represents homelessness and a forced nomadic existence.

Moore's three women are huddled together in purposeful communion (and are currently located in Battersea Park, London). They are made from a light Darley Dale stone, which was chosen because it would have weathered well in New York's sea air, as Moore originally intended to sell this piece to the Museum of Modern Art.

Parker's *Folkestone Mermaid* was conceived of both as a reinterpretation of one of the most popular tourist attractions in the world, Copenhagen's *Little Mermaid* (Eriksen, 1913), and as a means of engaging with Folkestone's local community as well as the reality of the female form. Inspired by the story *The Sea Lady* by H. G. Wells (a long-time resident of Folkestone), the mermaid's watchful gaze over the horizon is an allusion to the threat of rising sea levels and endangered populations living by the sea.

Decoy took the theme of 'Inside Out' (taking an 'inside' object out of context into the 'outside') quite literally, looking at the physical effect and changed poetic meaning in presenting an interior object in a state of vulnerability within the outside world. Von Weiler has worked in a variety of educational settings as an artist-in-residence, including mentoring post-16 pupils towards a public artwork in Newcastle in collaboration with Antony Gormley and working with deprived communities towards creating unique pieces born out of the voices of the community.

Another Place is a piece of modern sculpture by Sir Antony Gormley. It consists of 100 cast-iron figures facing towards the sea at Crosby beach, Merseyside. The figures are modelled on the artist's own naked body and are fully visible at low tide. The work proved controversial due to safety concerns and what some considered to be the 'offensive' nature of the naked statues.

Figure 3.11 Henry Moore, *Three Standing Figures*, 1947

Figure 3.12 Cornelia Parker, *The Folkestone Mermaid*, 2011

Figure 3.13 Carl von Weiler, *Decoy*, 2006

The Hive consists of 32 horizontal stacked layers of hexagonal geometry creating an abstracted analogue of a honeycomb. A rotational twist in the aluminium structure introduces movement, suggestive of a swarm. This interactive sculpture explores the life of the bee colony through an immersive multisensory experience. Visitors can walk inside and under the hive and interact with the continuous pulse of light and sound.

Ben Wilson is an artist better known by another name, 'The Chewing-Gum Man'. For more than a decade he has systematically turned over 10,000 trodden-in chewing gums that pepper the streets of London into miniature canvases. He has perfected

Figure 3.14 Antony Gormley, *Another Place*, 1997

Figure 3.15 Wolfgang Buttress, *The Hive*, 2016

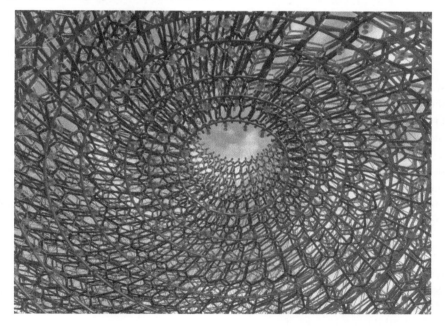

a technique using a blowtorch and layers of acrylic paint and lacquer to make tiny, shining works of art at our feet. His subject matter ranges from minuscule yet realistic London scenes to brightly coloured abstract patterns and strange creatures. This image shows one of the hundreds of his artworks on the Millennium Bridge in the heart of London and is seen as a sculptural adornment.

Figure 3.16 Ben Wilson, *Chewing Gum*, 2018

La Trabant, a painting by Birgit Kinder, features on a segment of the Berlin Wall showcased in The East Side Gallery in Berlin, the largest outdoor art gallery in the world. After the reunification of East and West Germany, this segment of the wall was made into a public gallery and various artists were invited to add their work to the wall's unadorned segments. This particular image commemorates not only the breaking of the wall in November 1989, but the ubiquitous Trabant (the car driven by most East Germans at the time).

Spanish artist Francisco Leiro creates freestanding life-size figures from polychrome wood. The sculpture shown here in can be found standing in a solitary position at the entrance to the Centro de Arte Contemporaneo de Malaga and reflects his continual investigation of the formal possibilities of figurative sculpture. Look closely at the apparently lifelike but physically impossible pose of this figure!

Natasha Morland draws inspiration from the great outdoors – walks through city parks, hikes through forests, journeys through the wilderness. She takes her visceral response to these surroundings as a starting point, often juxtaposing them with people in ambiguous ways. They become a contemplation of life's daily trials and tribulations – a meditative response to the inner workings of one's mind, with nature's unpredictability as the perfect backdrop.

Mei Ting Sze is a contemporary artist who explores the possibilities of ceramics. In her first solo exhibition, Sze continues to create a space of illusion through forging 'peculiar' objects in strong contrast with our ordinary environment. The shapes of the objects are unusual and in fluorescent colours. It is a dialogue not limited by language. It is about how objects 'speak' and have their ways with us in the space of illusion.

Figure 3.17 Birgit Kinder, *La Trabant*, 2011

Figure 3.18 Francisco Leiro, untitled sculpture, 2002

Figure 3.19 Natasha Morland, *Chorus Line*, 2018

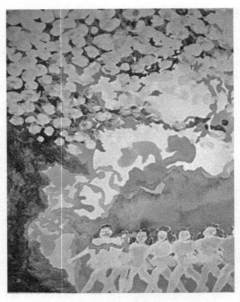

Figure 3.20 Mei Sze Ting, *Untitled*, 2017

Conclusion

Sometimes, the simple offer of an art session in the primary school classroom is itself irresistible for the majority of children. Whether it is a sign of our times and a reflection of the dearth of this subject with their school existence, or whether the trigger of interest relates to the very practical, active and expressive learning it requires, the fact remains that Art and Design, when taught well, is high up there in the irresistibility stakes. As suggested, the quality of equipment, unusual materials, prevocational artworks and an interested and engaged adult will make all the difference to how we motivate and intrigue the children we work with.

Perhaps the final words are best summarized by an eleven-year-old as she defined an irresistible art experience:

> When something is too tempting to ignore that you just have to try it out.
>
> (Maia, aged 11)

Recommended reading

The following three texts are suggested as follow-on reading:

Adams, E., (2003), *Drawing on Experience*. Hove: Drawing Power, The Big Campaign for Drawing.

Janes, K. (2014), *Using the Visual Arts for Cross-Curricular Teaching and Learning: Imaginative Ideas for the Primary School*. Oxford: Routledge.

Meager, N. (2012), *Teaching Art 4–7*. London: Belair.

Chapter 4
Art and Design as a Practical Activity

Within this chapter the notion of art and the practical nature of art will be discussed. One cannot really consider teaching within Art and Design without elements of practical activity. The consideration of the term 'practical', and its nature, will be explored in relation to specific activities involving, drawing, painting and sculpture. The following questions will be discussed:

- What counts as practical activity in Art and Design?
- Why should Art and Design involve practical activity, including drawing skills, the use of clay, paint and sculpture?
- What role does practical work play in primary school Art and Design?
- How does talk develop Art and Design as a practical activity?

What counts as practical activity in Art and Design?

When considering this question one must first consider what art is and why we teach it. This has been explored in more detail in Chapter 2, though it would be useful to briefly reflect here on art lessons, with special attention being paid to the practical elements. If asked to describe an art lesson, many teachers would probably focus on the practical nature of the activity, however, the practical element does not exist without cognitive engagement. Eisner (2002) suggests the notion of a 'work of art' can have two meanings. Firstly, it can refer to the product created, which children can observe, analyse and question and, secondly, it can refer to the 'work' element invested in the piece of art, referring to the process or journey of making the artwork as well as the decision-making process, itself involving elements of skill progression and imaginative or self-expressive energy (2002: 81). Both involve having a practical nature and both are key elements in the study of Art and Design.

As Eisner suggests:

> Artistry consists of having an idea worth expressing, the imaginative ability needed to conceive of how; the technical skills needed to work effectively with some

material, and the sensibilities needed to make the delicate adjustments that will give the forms the moving qualities that the best of them possess.

(Eisner, 2002: 81)

Within the National Curriculum (Department for Education (DfE), 2013) there is an expectation that practical considerations and an ability to analyse 'great artists' should occur, while a pupil is also mastering the skills and exploration of media leading to their ability to express personal ideas within the subject. These elements within the Art and Design curriculum are key to supporting the individual pupil beyond the practical elements. Hickman (2005) supports this, suggesting that the teaching of art not only allows skill development but can also promote key thinking skills, which can also be utilized further across the curriculum. Therefore, when teachers consider the practical elements in order to teach the technical skills, they should also consider wider opportunities for the exploration of ideas, and especially the encouragement of the use of the imagination and freedom of self-expression.

Why should Art and Design involve practical activity?

Later in this chapter we will consider this question through the use of case studies that focus on elements of drawing, painting and sculpture. These examples are by no means exhaustive and the reader, whether as a practicing or a student teacher, should consider reading further from the additional reading suggested at the end of the chapter.

Drawing

Drawing in its simplest form results from the ability to make marks that relate to each other and form an image. Children begin to make these marks from a very young age. As children develop, their marks start to relate to each other and then links between form and symbolism start to occur. (See Figure 4.1.)

Within the curriculum, drawing is not only important within the domain of Art and Design, Taylor suggested that, for a child, drawing is key to their understanding of their world. Drawing is a tool that supports the development of our ability to identify signs and symbols as well as enabling us to 'discover through seeing', whether through our own recorded images or that of another (Taylor, cited in Garner, 2008: 9). Drawing is also the earliest recording of human communication. The cave paintings from 30,000 years ago show Neolithic people communicating a record of themselves, the animals and other entities that played a significant role in their lives. Without these drawings our understanding of this historical time period would have been severely limited.

Figure 4.1 The First recordings in a sketchbook (child aged two years)

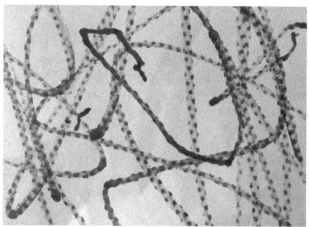

It is through the use of drawing, either with symbols or images, that children start to communicate their knowledge and then develop their understanding. Drawing in the early years continues to support the child's ability to communicate and express themselves when language or written words have not been fully mastered. This does not occur naturally in isolation but is interrelated with speech, play and the formulation of writing (Anning and Ring, 2004). Matthews (2003) suggested that the importance of drawing lies in that it enables a child to develop 'form representations, symbols and signs', which is the 'basis for all thinking' (2003: 1). Therefore, the act of engaging in drawing is of great benefit to a child – far beyond the boundary of the Art and Design curriculum. Cox (1992), Hope (2008) and Taylor (cited in Garner 2008) all see drawing as a tool for learning, supporting the child in exploring and investigating their ideas, using drawing as a visual tool for thinking through them, thus demonstrating the ability to solve problems in pictorial forms. This is a powerful skill and something children and adults engage in alike. For example, how often does the designer draw and redraw a design in order to eliminate or solve persistent problems? I experienced this recently, by drawing and redrawing design layouts for a new bathroom, the various challenges were observed and identified. The redrawing process addressed them in order to fully resolve them, but without this ability to draw and visualize the space, these problems could not have been addressed. The repeated drawing of the layout and design enabled the generation of many possibilities and options, from which an effective solution was found.

Taylor states that drawing is 'an investigative, transformative and generative tool' that supports the creation of ideas and concepts (Taylor, cited in Garner, 2008: 9). Clearly then drawing and thinking are particularly interrelated. Our current curriculum only identifies drawing specifically as a skill within the subject domain of Art and Design, stating that children should 'become proficient in drawing' (DfE, 2013: 1). What is termed or understood as proficient here is not clearly identified, although the Office for Standards in Education, Children's Services and Skills (Ofsted, 2009, 2012) identified drawing as an area not taught particularly effectively within schools currently. This is deeply regrettable and probably further reflects the limitations of the training of the teachers.

Children should be encouraged to draw for a range of reasons, not solely those relating to the mastery of the Art and Design curriculum. Adams (2011) suggests we use different forms of drawing and identifies four different purposes for drawing: perception, communication, invention and action. (The example given above of drawing a bathroom design clearly illustrates the notion of inventing, the creating something new, with the homeowner as a designer.) Drawing both enables and empowers a child to explore a range of areas within the curriculum, so teachers should consider carefully where drawing supports the wider curriculum. This will enable the child to communicate and understand new learning opportunities and therefore seize the potential of drawing as a tool for learning.

Quick pause moment – *Thinking about drawing*:

- Make a list of when you consciously plan for drawing to enable learning.
- Consider who uses drawing as an integral part of their job.
- When did you last draw to solve a problem?

Drawing is constantly used within the curriculum to engage pupils with their learning and help them to develop an understanding of difficult concepts. Consider how many times we might share an image with children to support their knowledge. For example, in maths we might encourage children to draw their problems using symbols or images to support their workings-out. In literacy, children are regularly encouraged to create a storyboard or draw visual plans to support and develop different forms of writing. While in science children can often be found drawing their observations of the world around them – visually recording their investigations. Drawing is a fundamental skill that supports learning across the whole curriculum, and teachers need to consciously plan to teach children drawing skills and support in their development.

Painting

Painting, like drawing, has been a human activity for thousands of years. By painting on the walls of caves, humans have expressed their lives through paint and painted images. Through the engagement with paintings over time we can still learn much about our world history and culture.

If you could say it in words, there would be no reason to paint.

(Edward Hopper, 1882–1967)

From a young age children are actively encouraged to explore paint as a form of self-expression – a way to communicate their thoughts and feelings through the image-making process. The painting station is often a permanent fixture in an early years setting, or Reception classroom, with children having the opportunity to paint freely as the moment takes them. Unfortunately, as the need to communicate through the more generally acceptable formal written form starts to take precedence in classrooms for the following year groups, the opportunities for painting become increasingly thin on the ground.

Quick pause moment – *Thinking about painting*:

- What are your experiences of using paint either as a child or adult?
- What elements of painting have you seen or taught in the classroom?
- How are children's skills developed with paint? What are these skills?

Painting can support children to develop an understanding a range of concepts, such as tone, colour and composition as well as an understanding of the qualities and skills of paint application. For children to be able to fully develop these concepts, guidance and modelling from the teacher is necessary. The planning of painting activities requires careful thought to ensure children are exposed to a wide range of different kinds of paints (powder, ready-mixed, block, acrylic, etc.), thereby giving them the freedom to paint on a range of subjects and with a range of results.

Painting enables children to learn about colour through the mixing of paint and its application onto a chosen surface, as well as by observing the relationships of one colour with another. Cox and Watts state 'colour can be a great source of enjoyment and provides a powerful language to express responses to the world' (2007: 39). Young children should have the opportunity to explore a range of paints in a variety of colours. Classroom practitioners should teach children to mix colours and provide opportunities for children to explore colour independently. In schools where adults lack confidence with this, we have noted that money is often invested in buying the full range of ready-mixed paints and pupils consequently miss out on the learning opportunities offered through mixing their own colours. As children move into KS1 and beyond, their understanding of colour mixing can be extended further by introducing further skills and technical vocabulary. Children need to have an understanding of the names of colours, be able to identify the primary colours (red, yellow, blue) and be able to know the secondary colours and which colours to mix to create them.

Primary colours: red (magenta), yellow, blue (cyan)

Secondary colours:

orange = red + yellow
green= yellow + blue
purple = red + blue

Tertiary colours are a mix of primary and secondary colours and the proportions used control the colours obtained

The relationship between colours, light and visual perception should be appreciated by all pupils before they leave primary school. Knowing how to construct and use a colour wheel as well appreciate the difference between varieties of blue hues (e.g. cyan, royal and navy) will be extremely useful as the pupils develop. (For teachers who aren't sure themselves we would recommend obtaining Martin Wenham's (2003) book on art-based subject knowledge.)

For primary school children creating a rich variety of colours it is necessary to consider the amount of each colour added to the mix to enable them to create a colour recipe for their work. This enables them to develop their understanding of colour and expand the palette of colour choices available to them. Colours can be changed further through the addition of black or white (the addition of black creating shades, and of white creating tints). Children should also be introduced to the notion of complementary colours, these are colours that are opposite each other on the colour wheel, such as red and green or blue and orange, a little of the complementary colour within a painting or design makes the other colour really sing out. Artists consciously select colour combinations to create expressions of feelings or emotions – for example, the vibrancy of complementary colours can express joyfulness. Vincent Van Gogh, within his later work, can be seen to constantly play around with and explore complementary colours. Children could explore a number of his works and see how he used colours to explore and express different meanings, ensuring they look beyond *The Starry Night* (1889) or *Sunflowers* (1889), perhaps also looking at images such as *Wheatfield with Crows* (1890) or *Flowering Plum Orchard* (1887). Complementary colours can also be used to create a further range of shades (instead of the light-absorbing varieties made by adding black).

Analogous colours are a group of three of the colours next to each other on the colour wheel, with one being the dominant colour. Analogous use of colour can be more muted and calming in approach even when using shades of colour within a painting.

Children can be encouraged to look for these complementary colours or analogous colours used in a range of artists' or designers' work, for example Paul Klee, Georgia O'Keefe, Andy Warhol or David Hockney. Children need opportunities to explore colour mixing so both the equipment and freedom for this to happen should be incorporated into the lesson. When selecting resources for the painting lesson, consider creating opportunities for colour exploration, providing children (at times at least) with a limited palette from which they can mix some colours. This can be extended with challenges for mixing secondary and tertiary colours as well as shades and tints.

Expression through paint

When learning about paint it is useful to observe and learn from other artists, both contemporary and historical, as well as from other cultures and places. Children can begin to understand the way different artists use both paint and colour to communicate knowledge, symbolism and express emotions.

> Very young children may draw what they know, but it is said that they paint what they feel.
>
> (Barnes, 2015: 79)

If children can explore how artists use paint to express their thoughts and feelings it can encourage and empower them to then communicate their own emotions. It can also enable them to explore and play with the paint, often leading to their own discovery and invention of new techniques or colour schemes. The following is a case study exploring the experimental nature of one artist, Jessica Warboys, and her use of paint.

CASE STUDY: CURIOUS SEA PAINTING

Quick pause moment

Visiting the Tate St Ives gallery with a young girl aged seven (with the aim of just engaging with the gallery), the child was fascinated and curious about the work of artist Jessica Warboys in her exhibition 'The Studio and the Sea' (2017).

Warboys' large-scale works are influenced by the British coast and landscape, with this exhibition, consisting of two large-scale commissioned works, inspired by the Cornish landscape. The painting that particularly captured the child's attention was *Sea Painting, Zennor* (2015). The child was captivated because of two elements: firstly the size and scale of the painting (over 5 metres wide) and secondly the method the artist used, which could be described as non-traditional.

Warboys, in order to create these paintings, worked in the landscape itself like many artists, dating back to the Impressionists. She takes this a step even further by using the sea itself as a medium for the painting, which is a technique that she often follows in her work. Warboys casts natural pigments onto large sea-dampened canvases then submerges the pieces into the sea, allowing the water to intermingle and dance across the canvas shifting pigment at will, allowing sand, sea and the elements of Zennor to play their role in the creation of the final piece. This process fascinated the child, who later when using watercolours herself, was observed to be scattering or spraying paint across her paper, exploring the style and re-creating, in her view, the artist's technique. By placing expansive washes of colour across the page she almost let the water become the sea. This happened without direction or instruction. (See Figures 4.2 and 4.3.)

Figures 4.2 and 4.3 Responses by a seven-year-old

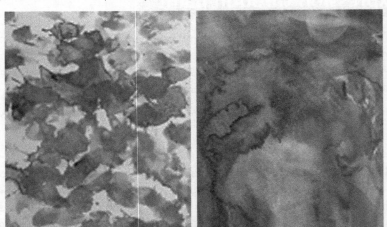

Tutchell (2014) suggests teachers should indulge children in these moments of inspiration and support further opportunities for sensory-based engagement. How might the child have developed their painting if actually given access to the sea or water?

There are some additional important points to consider.

Firstly, there is the understanding of the process, and how this can be applied very differently from artist to artist. This can only be gained through observing and studying a range of artists. Then children start to understand the range of processes that can be utilized.

Secondly, there is the opportunity for sensory exploration with paint. For the child to truly understand a paint's potential then exploration is vitally necessary. At times the exploration should be the sole focus, with greater importance than either imagery or content. Presenting the child with opportunities to explore a range of paints could have developed the child's thinking further. By providing opportunities to explore texture by adding everyday materials, such as sand, glue and glitter, the experience could be extended even further.

How might the child's experience have been enhanced still further if given the opportunity to also create their own work outside in the landscape itself, as Warboys herself did?

Sculpture

Sculpture enables children to develop their understanding of the three-dimensional objects, in particular the qualities of form, space and surface (Clough, 2007). The understanding of this notion and the language relating to this form is an element children struggle to fully grasp without both visual and tactile experiences. Clough goes on to suggest three-dimensional art forms have limited exposure in the primary classroom, something that our own experience supports. Children tend to have far greater access to drawing and painting but are provided with fewer opportunities with pieces that explore these three-dimensional qualities.

Quick pause moment – *Thinking about sculpture*:

- What is sculpture?
- Where did you last see a piece of sculpture?
- What material was it made from?
- What sculpture have you seen in school?

Three-dimensional art forms enable 'unique visual, formal and tactile languages' to develop when exploring the concept of form (Cox and Watts, 2007: 55). Teachers can enable children to understand the concept of form and the relationship between space and form. Children (and adults too), are often more aware of the positive, or concrete, elements of the form rather than the space around the form. Teachers can encourage children through their observations and guided discussion to consider both the form and the space surrounding it and the interplay between positive and negative space. Sculpture has many forms and can often be found outside in public spaces, as well as within galleries and museums. (See Figures 4.4 and 4.5.)

Accessibility to such pieces enable children to respond to art in situ, which can be a very powerful sensory experience. The tactile nature of this type of art often encourages involuntary exploration through touch and engagement with all the senses. Children can explore the use of the materials, texture, form and space, as such concepts cannot always be fully appreciated without first-hand experience.

Sculpture helps children to understand their three-dimensional world, and there are many materials that can be used to enable this exploration (see also Chapter 8). Materials such as clay or 'junk' for modelling are commonly found within the primary classroom. Other materials such as willow withies (thin branches from the willow tree) or Modroc (plaster of Paris impregnated bandage) are seen less often within schools. This is perhaps due to a lack of funding for the Art and Design curriculum or the teachers' absence of confidence in (or knowledge about) the use of such materials.

Sculpture can be effective in enabling children to understand the concept of form using very simple materials found within the school, such as card, paper or other recycled materials. There are a number of contemporary sculpture artists working with card

Figures 4.4 and 4.5 Public art sculpture comes in many forms

and paper, pushing the boundaries with complex structures – for example, Richard Sweeney's *Olympic Horse* (2012) demonstrates the possibilities of such an everyday material. Other contemporary artists such as Jen Stark or Valérie Buess also explore paper both in different ways, experimenting with colour and form. Their work demonstrates that even paper or card can be used to form large and complex sculptures.

CASE STUDY: WILLOW FORMS

The use of willow sculptures is an interesting way for children to explore their environment, and the work of land artists such as Andy Goldsworthy, Richard Long, Nancy Holt and Robert Smithson can be used as a stimulus or starting point to inspire children to create large-scale pieces of their own. These artists work mainly with natural materials and their work is often sited firmly in the landscape where seasonal changes interplay with the art form.

The willow sculptures shown here (Figures 4.6 and 4.7) were created by a class of Year 5 children exploring the concept of space and form in the natural environment. They were working alongside a contemporary artist Sue Shaw during one term.

Firstly, they developed an understanding of form by making small scale sculptures using straws and paper. The children then moved on to consider the properties of the willow and the challenges – what was possible and achievable with such material. The children worked collaboratively to respond to, and change the landscape using a mix of natural and man-made materials, each design and creation was worked on by a group of at least three children enabling them to hold bend and manipulate the willow.

The brief was to create different willow forms based on the human figure. The sculptures had to be large scale and have the ability to sit within the landscape for some time to come. Each figure was set into engineering bricks and embedded in the ground, which gave the children a stable base from which to work. The willow was soaked in water for a few days prior to use, to ensure the withies were pliable and easy to use. Children had to consider health and safety elements and all tools were both discussed and demonstrated. Protective eye wear was worn throughout the project. The children could add a range of materials to the sculpture or change and add more willow over a period of time. (See Figures 4.6 and 4.7.)

Figures 4.6 and 4.7 Willow forms

CASE STUDY: HORN BLASTER

The case study highlights a project where the children were working collaboratively to form a large-scale horn sculpture. They were exploring the ideas of sound-makers with artist Matt Rowe, who was himself working alongside other artists in developing a contemporary horn installation as part of The Folkestone Triennial 2017.

The children were eight to nine years old, and had not experienced a vast range of art activities before this point and had very limited experience with sculpture; therefore this project was identified as supporting the children with an experience that could help them develop new skills and understanding while also expressing their own ideas. They worked alongside the contemporary artist Matt Rowe on a range of workshops called 'Seeing with sound', which culminated in a collaborative installation.

Matt Rowe is contemporary ceramic artist but, like many artists, Matt works with a range of materials and uses a significant amount of technology. One interesting aspect of sculpture is the way materials and processes can interact to develop a piece or build the notion of an installation. This ability to mix

Figures 4.8 and 4.9 Horns created by the children and the final installation

media and develop a process to create and collaborate over an installation is particularly powerful for children. It can also mirror the way some contemporary artists are working today and allow children to explore this. The 'Seeing with sound' workshops enabled the children to develop pictures that related to the cosmic universe, as a first step, and then communicate with the virtual space. The children worked on large-scale collaborative drawings of outer space using a range of coloured neon markers. These drawings were photographed and the artist working with the children turned the photos into sound representations that were shared with the children.

The children explored the notion of turning their drawings into photographs, which were then turned into soundscapes. The children then made cosmic horns to blast sounds into outer space, using card and tape, and guided by the artist, who had already made some decisions about materials and colour, including the need to use neon throughout in order to ensure continuity in the final installation. Once children had created the structures of their horns, they could make their own choices of selecting colours and patterns to express their individuality.

Then the children developed their creations further using their horns to create sounds that were recorded onto software. The software allowed their sounds to be represented as images, and thus children started to understand the concept of sound waves and the differences that can occur with pitch and tone, a particularly useful element of cross-curricular learning. The last step was for the children to use their horns to develop a final installation, which was constructed from the images of sounds and the horns. This clearly collaborative piece of sculpture used a range of media and technology and enabled every child's work to be included and thus valued. Working alongside the artist enabled the children to observe the processes he used within his own work to develop new ways of seeing art and the relationship between art and technology.

It also enabled the children to ask questions about why he wanted to be an artist and what it was like. The potential to develop the project further could be endless with many aspects of cross-curricular work that could have been developed. There were obvious links with the notion of sound and how sound travels leading to how humans hear. But more than this was the creative thinking around the technology and the manipulation of materials from the visual to the notion of sound.

What role does practical work play in primary Art and Design?

The practical elements within the Art and Design lesson are central to the process. As already highlighted, without the practical elements a child is not able to engage with the skills needed. But from our perspective as teachers this does not mean they have any less academic rigour. As Ogier points out 'Art and Design is every inch an intellectual activity, as [well as] a practical one' (2017: 38). The practical engages the creative thinking, the invention and exploration. Without the practical elements such as manipulating materials the child will fail to fully understand the potential of the materials. A child cannot fully master the potential of clay by the analysis of an artist's work or by a simple transmission of knowledge. There is a real need to touch and manipulate materials first hand, thus giving a greater understanding of the medium, which in turn allows the child to raise questions such as:

- What happens if … [with a variety of possible endings]?
- How will it dry?
- Can I add paint to the clay?
- Will my model stand? If not, how can I make it stand?
- Why is the material sticky?
- How can I … ?

Eisner (1997) suggests that children can only really understand certain aspects of Art and Design by coming into direct contact with materials and by utilizing their senses to support their cognitive development. Only through experience of such contact with media such as paint, chalk or Modroc, for example, can a child develop a truly secure foundation of understanding such a material. This, in turn, enables pupils with their creative thinking to then utilize the material's potential; and it can also ensure that the outcomes show elements of originality and experimentation rather than a more generic 'colour- or sculpt-by-numbers' exercise. These practical elements within Art and Design lessons could be seen as linked to the notion of play – the ability to explore the potential of the different media, to experiment and to investigate. The processes themselves develop the child's thinking and enable them to challenge ideas, thus encouraging communication and sharing, with each other or their teacher, the small inventions or discoveries made. Without the practical elements of Art and Design lessons, the subject can become simply an appreciation of previous artists' work. We need to carefully consider the question as to whether children really can appreciate something that they have not explored or experimented with themselves? Can a child understand the investment or challenges the artist might have endured if they themselves have not experienced similar? We would argue that it is like understanding the taste of a cool fresh watermelon sprinkled with salt: you can be told how mouthwateringly and refreshingly sweet it is, but you cannot really appreciate it until you taste it for yourself. Art is similar, as the engagement enables the child to gain both cognitive growth and the opportunity of mastery of the subject.

How does talk develop in Art and Design as a practical activity?

Talk can take different forms in an Art and Design lesson, the 'teacher talk' explaining, questioning and hypothesizing the children's enquiries – observing, questioning, expressing or simply fulfilling a need. But what has been clear from recent research is that talk supports children's development of their knowledge and understanding (Corden, 2000). Bruner (1986) identifies that talking ideas through consolidates and develops children's understanding, enabling them to make sense of new ideas or concepts. It is therefore important that, within the Art and Design lesson, teachers develop frequent opportunities for the children to talk about the resources they are exploring, to ask questions and to comment on artists' work, while also having rich opportunities to reflect and explain their own works of art. Meager (2012) suggests that a child's art is a form of communication and one that can support them in communicating their thoughts effectively. The practical activity of art can stimulate and encourage powerful talk, aiding children's understanding and thus supporting them in their ability to communicate in all modes. For teachers, it is important to enable the child to communicate their ideas verbally in order to give meaning to their work, otherwise we may misunderstand or come to incorrect conclusions about the child's artwork. The adult's interpretation of an artwork can be very different to the child's intended meaning, as discussed in the case study below.

CASE STUDY: A SIX-YEAR-OLD'S PAINTING

The child covers the whole piece of paper with black paint leaving only a strip of white showing.

At first glance, this may seem very dark and, in some way, almost menacing. It may even concern an inexperienced teacher.

By taking time to discuss the work with the child, an entirely different perspective can be appreciated. In this instance (a true story) the boy explained both why it was so dark and why he had made such a creation. The child simply explained that the picture was of a badger and they only come out at night – and, consequently, you only see flashes of white. The fact that the animal couldn't be identified, of course, did not mean that it was not present, but the conversation enabled the teacher to appreciate and better assess the child's painting, his expression and understanding.

This demonstrates the importance of talking with children about their work as it adds meaning for the observer, informing them of the knowledge and understanding the child holds, as well as giving insights into their creativity. In this way, it also supports the identification of areas for future potential learning.

Children should have plenty of opportunities to talk and discuss artists and their artworks. Sharing their thoughts, feelings and understanding of a particular work can both inform and support rich learning across the curriculum. Sometimes, artworks can be intimidating – for many of us (including children) – so we need to find ways to assist the growth of confidence. Children need to be empowered with a sense of freedom, so that they feel they can question and comment on work without teachers expecting or searching for what they deem (or otherwise believe) to be the right answer. Art speaks differently to all of us so the answers, and questions, will be different for each individual (Barbe-Gall, 2005).

Consider what questions you would have had as a child when confronted with the *Mona Lisa* by Leonardo da Vinci. What elements do you think would stand out for a child? What elements stand out to you as a teacher?

Quick pause moment – *Thinking about the effect art has on you*:

- What was the last artwork you looked at?
- What questions came to mind?
- What feelings did it evoke in you?

When talking about artwork, the questions who, what, where, when, why and how are a useful way to start investigating a painting (Ogier, 2017). These questions can support and offer a framework that the children can use in their conversations with each other about art works. Encourage children to give justifications for their answers. It is not enough to say I like this sculpture: What element is it that you like? And why is that? Perhaps it is the form, texture, feeling or expressive nature of the artwork.

Talk becomes a vital aspect when encouraging children to develop their art both individually and collaboratively. Both Barbe-Gall (2005, 2012) and Gregory (2005, 2013, 2015) highlight that talk is an essential part of the practical element of creating, allowing children to discuss their explorations; and sharing discoveries enables them to become skilled in new areas. Children should have the opportunity to explore the different media and techniques; and talking about and demonstrating new methods can develop their knowledge and understanding of materials as well as supporting their motivation, self-confidence and ability to take risks.

Recommended reading

The following four texts are suggested as follow-on reading:

Addison, N. (2011), 'Moments of Intensity: Affect and the Making and Teaching of Art.'
    International Journal of Art and Design in Education, 30(3), pp. 363–78.
Clough, P. (2007), *Sculptural Materials in the Classroom.* London: A&C Black Publishers.
Rowntree, J. and Hooson, D. (2018), *Clay in Common.* Axminster, Triarchy Press.
Hafeli, M. (2014), *Exploring Studio Materials: Teaching Creative Art Making to Children.*
    New York: Oxford University Press.

Chapter 5
Skills to Develop in Art and Design

This chapter introduces the types of skills developed through engaging in Art and Design, explores how they can be used in the classroom, and considers their importance in the learning process. The learning process itself includes the skills of critical thinking, exploration, creativity and personal expression, which are discussed in relation to practice. We also consider the distinct nature of the sketchbook, exploring how such 'books' can be used within the primary classroom and in turn support the Art and Design process.

The following areas are addressed:

- What are the process skills within Art and Design?
- Why are process skills important?
- What skills should teachers start with?
- How do skills enable the child's autonomy?
- The role of the sketchbook throughout the process

What are the skills within Art and Design?

When considering the skills related to Art and Design as a subject, it is important to understand that there are two skill sets to consider. Firstly, the process skills used for developing or creating any art form or enabling the engagement with art; and, secondly, there are specific material skills relating to the use of different media (for example charcoal, paint or clay). This second skill set could be referred to as a technical skill set.

This chapter focuses specifically on the first set of skills, which are referred to as process skills for Art and Design. Children develop these skills by engaging with the Art and Design process through exploring, experimenting, making, reflecting and appraising their work. These process skills in fact underpin all aspects of the Art and Design curriculum and are further evident across the arts in general.

This chapter focuses on the following skills;

- Invention
- Analysis

- Expression
- Imagination
- Observation.

Quick pause moment – *Thinking about skills in Art and Design*:

- When do you as a teacher use the skills listed above?
- Are some of these more important than others?
- How can we develop these skills – for ourselves as well as for our pupils?

Process skills can be developed within Art and Design regardless of the medium, subject or content, although consideration of these skills at different stages can both support and enhance the actual process development. For process skills to impact on the child's developing knowledge they should form part of a sequence of activities that enables the child to engage in different elements. One might also consider that these skills can be developed not solely within Art and Design, but also within other curriculum subjects – and even beyond the arts.

We know that art is currently a marginalized subject within the curriculum (National Society for Education in Art and Design (NSEAD), 2016) often not recognized for enabling the skills identified above, skills that support the child's cognitive development. Instead art is too often seen as a complementary vehicle to service other subjects or as a product to enhance the classroom environment. But creative skills should not be overlooked, as they are fundamentally linked to human development itself. Read's (1943) early curriculum model identified the importance of self-expression, observation and appreciation, which are still reflected in the current National Curriculum (Department for Education (DfE), 2013). In fact, creative thinking is repeatedly identified within the National Curriculum, and the skills within Art and Design are included as invention. However, both imagination and analysis are also key to the development process. The skills involved in critical observation or analysis of an existing painting or sculpture enable the child to enquire – questioning and developing an understanding of form, structure, composition and meaning of the artwork – and so develop learning on many levels. Consider a child observing a form such as the human hand, there is much to understand regarding both shape and form. Vincent van Gogh spent many years grappling over just this problematic challenge, drawing, redrawing and observing, each time trying to gain a more realistic image. Indeed, there are many artists in whom we can observe such a struggle. Identifying and sharing these struggles is important as children need to understand and know that artists have to continually analyse and develop their thinking. Artists don't just record what they'd like to record – there are a series of challenges and cognitive difficulties to work through.

Critical thinking enables us to question the processes within the art form, or to develop an understanding of the historical context or statements conveyed within it.

Observing Gainsborough's portrait *Mr and Mrs Andrews* (1750) could lead to questions about the sitters, the landscape and the compositional relationships between the two, while also exploring the process involved within the portrait. Therefore, the Art and Design National Curriculum (DfE, 2013) still affords children the opportunity to develop the range of skills identified above, which supports them across subjects to question, imagine, evaluate and invent. This is one of the paths to mastery for those teachers willing to find their way through the somewhat confusing wording of the National Curriculum document itself.

Barnes (2015) identifies the importance of young children becoming visually literate in order to enable them to understand the world they live in. These identified skills form part of the development of that visual literacy. In today's society, images play a key role in communicating with the world and much media is image-based and likely to become more so. Therefore the importance of children developing strong visual literacy has never been as important as it is today in the twenty-first century. Hickman (2005) considers visual literacy as an ability to develop knowledge and understanding of visual forms that relate to our culture or heritage. This continues throughout childhood and into adulthood, and as culture changes so do our reference points as our knowledge of visual forms builds. Images and the use of colour play an important role in the visual world and are used regularly in advertising and news items to evoke an emotional response from viewers. Images can portray more powerful emotions than words – for example, the famous Pulitzer Prize-winning picture *Saigon Execution* (1968) by Eddie Adams instils utter fear and brutality into the soul of the observer, leaving a sick empty feeling wondering why and what actually happened? Although first encountered many years ago, this image still evokes that same emotional response today. When Adams commented years later about the impact of his image, he said that 'still photographs are the most powerful weapon in the world' (Adams, 2001). I would agree with his sentiment but would argue that the truth extends beyond photos into the world of art: it potentially has the power to fully engage our thinking and provoke questions of our perceptions of the world.

Process skills

Although in the teaching of Art and Design many skills overlap, those identified above will be individually considered with reference to other curriculum subjects – for example how the skills of analysis might be further supported through History or Science.

Invention

Invention clearly relates to the notion of making – the making of something new, for example something tangible and concrete, such as a model or a drawing. This could also be said to include the invention of a new process. The process of inventing may involve engaging with other processes such as analysis, observation or imagination. This process of invention is deemed a key skill in the National Curriculum (DfE, 2013), which highlights that an overall aim is for children to become creative thinkers and that they should enjoy the act of making or creating.

The idea of invention is closely linked to that of creativity and it is worth briefly considering what is understood by the term creativity. The National Advisory Committee on Creative and Cultural Education report *All Our Futures* (Department for Education and Employment (DfEE), 1999) stated that creativity is an 'imaginative activity fashioned so as to produce outcomes that are both original and of value' (p. 29). Creativity is not solely the domain of the arts, although undoubtedly the development of skills through the arts has a major impact on a child's ability to be creative. By encouraging children to be inventive they can become truly creative – by pushing boundaries and extending their thinking beyond their experiences. If children are to invent, they must have both the opportunity and the freedom to explore, and to take risks with ideas and materials, in order to consider potentials in new and different ways. Without such opportunities children may lack the skills, experience and understanding required for the creativity needed in order to lead to the skill of invention. If a child is to invent, then exploration of materials is a central element, as are the abilities to play with, to experiment with and to try out ideas, which lead children to discover, make new marks, paint and create, and produce objects in different ways. Figure 5.1 demonstrates this freedom of experimentation in operation. This

Figure 5.1 Child investigating a range of marks

child is printing or mark-making with a corn-on-the-cob, delighting in the different patterns created on the surface of the paper. As teachers we need to offer and adapt such experiences frequently throughout the early years.

Analysis

The ability to analyse within Art and Design is a crucial skill for many reasons. Firstly, the National Curriculum currently requires children to have an understanding of 'great artists, architects and designers' (DfE, 2013: 177). This is not a new requirement as there has been an expectation for children to know and understand about artists and cultures across the world since the first National Curriculum document was published (Department of Education and Science (DES), 1992). However, the term 'great artist, architects and designers' is not a clearly defined one, which leaves it open to different interpretations by schools and teachers. Do schools perceive greatness to be contemporary or does greatness only come with historical importance, therefore are we constraining teachers to only consider famous individuals from history? Currently, how is the concept of greatness perceived by teachers and children? Are we as educators exploring this notion while equipping children with the skills of analysis? After all, what makes a great artist? And for that matter, what is art?

Recently, the seven-year-old daughter of one of the authors adamantly stated that photography was *not* art. This was firmly fixed in her understanding as she responded 'painting, sculpture and drawing are art'. This view is worth exploring with both teachers and children, as the defined boundaries of the subject domain will have major implications for both teaching and learning. Is it also possible that the greatness of those who make art comes only with some form of recognition, historical importance or even the mastery of skills? Perhaps a combination is necessary? Can you only be a great artist if you paint, draw or sculpt? There is an underlying assumption of elitism that we want to challenge, as it severely limits our understanding and experience of art to a historic, Western perspective and fails to acknowledge today's position (Chalmers, 1999).

A child's ability to analyse might enable them to consider and articulate such questions as greatness, but how might teachers develop these analytical skills? The teacher's role in supporting effective analysis is central – whether this is in supporting the child's analysis of and reflection on an artist, designer, craft-maker, architect or the child's own work. The teacher should encourage children to make observations of their own and others work by equipping them with skills for analysis, reflection and evaluation as well as an ability to make effective comparisons (Buchanan, 1995 cited in Robinson, 2011). The teacher, in developing such skills, needs to take the opportunities to both model and practise them in relation to their own work and the work of others. By doing so, the children in turn will become more confident and be able to express their own ideas, ask questions, prompt reflections and share their own views. The National Gallery offers teachers the opportunity each year to focus in depth on one particular painting with a programme called 'Take One Picture'. A very useful element of this programme is the structured resources publication for teachers, available on the National Gallery website, which can be used to support an analysis of the image, including historical background information about the painting (although not limited to this aspect alone). The resources suggest questions to ask the children, in order to elicit feelings and thoughts and to develop knowledge and understanding. Children are also encouraged to develop their own creative responses to the artwork using different media and art forms, allowing them to move a long way beyond producing a simple pastiche of the artist's work (Cox & Watts, 2007). The skilled and knowledgeable teacher who has mastered this can encourage analysis of the artwork, enabling questioning, observation, and the expression of feelings and views, and utilize these into creative art-making activities. The child's analysis informs and empowers their own creative process, which leads them away from a limiting copy, as Cox & Watts (2007) suggests, into a more original piece of their own (Barnes, 2015). The analysis should focus on the subject matter alongside that of process. For example: How did the artist develop the work? What materials have they used? How did they create the image or sculpture? What can we learn from this and use within our work? What message was the artist conveying? How does it make us (as the viewer) feel? Children should develop the skills to question art forms at deep levels in order to gain some understanding of both how and why the work was produced, including an awareness of the historical context at the time the artwork was created. In some literature this is referred to as critical and contextual studies.

We believe that art is about being curious. The art form and the analysis should capture our visual interest. The curiosity about who made it, why, what's happening, what it is, should lead us as viewers to discover the meaning within the artwork. Artworks are often provocative, demanding a response from the observer. Banksy (a contemporary artist), for example, is known for his political and social commentary on current topical issues, such as his 2017 image (see Figure 5.2) situated in Dover, Kent. This image of the European flag with one yellow star being chipped off, represents the ongoing political process of leaving the European Union ('Brexit') – it engages the viewer to reflect.

Banksy is insisting that the viewer stops and thinks. Although such images have many aesthetic qualities, the chief aim is to elicit a response, feeling or thought around a current political issue. Banksy's image has a very different role to say Monet's famous series of paintings *Water Lilies* (1918), some of which were created for the French nation to evoke an emotional response: to give a sense of a calm haven, of peace for the country of France after the turmoil of the First World War. Children should be supported in exploring a wider understanding of why art is produced. It is through using these skills of analysis that we can encourage children to be reflective, to question and evaluate the processes artists go through, as well as the processes they can develop within their own work, while also considering the place for art within our own society. In this way, the experiences of art gained while at primary school are part of a richer, longer-lasting legacy as the children prepare for life in the later years of this century.

Teachers need to give careful consideration to the choice of art forms shared with children. Currently schools spend much time focusing on well-known paintings,

Figure 5.2 Banksy 2017 (Dover, Kent)

mainly from secondary sources, often in digital or printed form. This diet of second-ary images can impact on the ability of successful analysis. How can children explore the questions identified above without at times experiencing art at first hand? The size and scale of such images can often be lost when viewed from a secondary source. Let's take, for example, Lubaina Himid's 2017 Turner Prize winning *A Fashionable Marriage* (2017). Once reproduced, it is difficult to appreciate either the scale or materials of the original image. The original experienced first-hand provides an understanding of the three dimensional nature of the cut-out sections, the impressive size and also the range of materials utilized. Without first-hand observation one might miss many of these aspects. Understanding such elements of scale and medium adds much to the observer's analysis, thus impacting on the production of their own art-works. This would suggest the need for children and teachers to have opportunities to engage first-hand with art forms, either through a gallery visit or other first-hand opportunities. Imagine all the smells, tactile experiences from touching and the sounds heard by using this approach: they are almost impossible to evoke from a reproduced image – whether a small postcard or a larger digital image projected in the classroom.

Expression

Children need to have both the skills and the confidence to express themselves. Art should afford and grant children the skills to express themselves, creating artworks that reflect unique aspects of themselves. Too often, from our experience, the art seen on display in schools seems to focus on the creation of thirty perfect images with little sign of individualism, instead a replication of an artist's work or perhaps a teacher's idea. The ability to express oneself is the mark of an excellent art lesson or experience, where children have the confidence and skill required to demonstrate the realization of their own creation. Eisner (1997) believed that a key purpose of art being taught in schools was to support self-expression, while developing the academic (child), through observation of the world. Eisner here is identifying growth in two areas; firstly, self-realization of the inner self understanding of who we are and what is important to us as individuals, and, secondly, the academic knowledge of all the elements within art. In turn this enables the child to develop their creative thinking skills, impacting across a number of components of the curriculum.

For children to develop the skill of self-expression it is necessary to be able to read and understand different forms of expression. This is, in fact, something the child has been doing from the moment they were born, reading cues such as facial expression and tone of voice alongside more complex expressions used in language or imagery. Next is the ability to express themselves in an artistic outcome of some sort. For this one also needs to master the skills required for the medium in order to enable effective expression. Eisner (1997) suggests that if the child is without such skills and ability to manage the medium, then their artistic expression cannot be fulfilled. In view of this, teachers should ensure children have opportunities to explore different media alongside developing an understanding of how to use them effectively. Different materials have varying characteristics and capabilities, and children need some experience and understanding of what these are as well as being able to consider unknown possibilities. In many ways, this is not dissimilar to the knowledge needed to understand a mathematical concept. Without the mathematical concept, such as fractions, being taught, children do not automatically have the capability to solve problems or express their mathematical understanding. So the exploration of materials is a vital element of classroom art – especially allowing children a personal choice of materials. Without the opportunity to manage and select their materials and media, the child may not achieve the ability to express themselves fully (Robinson, 1995; Eisner, 1997). Children need to develop their control or mastery of the medium, which can be quite a challenge within the limited curriculum time allocated for art as already noted. However, teachers sometimes lack confidence themselves, and this can result in a curriculum that offers narrow experiences and ultimately insufficient knowledge for the child to use well (Gregory, 2005). Perhaps the curriculum would do better by focusing on exploring fewer media, thereby allowing them time to develop a mastery of the materials in order to aid the development of the children's expressive abilities.

As already stated, children need confidence in their own ability to express themselves and so to value their own ideas and the work they produce. In this way, art empowers their voice or channel for personal and social communication. Hickman suggests the child can develop an understanding of self 'through the exploration of personal ideas and feelings' (2005: 49). This process plays an important role in the child's development of self-esteem enabling them to explore and ultimately express complex issues in a more confident manner. The notion of expression and 'personal growth' of the child are clearly related, and without an understanding of self and personal confidence then elements of personal expression are unlikely to occur (Hickman, 2005: 51). We would suggest that, for the teacher, enabling the child to be confident in expressing their ideas is more nuanced and challenging than the mastery of skills. This is where engagement with artists' work, both historical and contemporary, is pivotal, as an analysis of the artist's expression can provide and amplify the child's voice and develop their ability to personalize the responses they choose to make.

Imagination

Eisner (2002) would suggest that 'much of what is important in the arts depends upon the use of the imagination, the ability to engage students' imagination is a critically important skill in art teaching' (2002: 53). Teachers may perceive that children find it easy to access and utilize their imaginations – think of the notion of the innocent child with endless imagination, just ready to be tapped into. However, in our experience of teaching art, the imagination can often take some stimulation – it does not automatically fire up on demand. As an adult, consider being faced with the task of being expected to produce a drawing from your imagination without any stimulus and within a set period of time. This is such a complex and daunting task. How challenging, and possibly frustrating, might this activity be? Yet this is often the scenario presented to children and, unsurprisingly, it may lead to disengagement and ultimately loss of confidence within art itself. A child's capacity to be imaginative relies on their ability to 'recombine stored and recalled mental images to form new ones' (Robinson, 1995: 130). This highlights the importance for children to observe and explore a diverse range of images from the real world, such as landscapes, objects from their environment or images from a variety of cultures or artists and designers. Salvador Dali is known for his highly imaginative surrealist artworks. When appraising Dali's *Swans Reflecting Elephants* (1937), observation meets the imagination, as this painting could not have been produced without very careful observation of both elephants and swans. It is only through this combination from the observed that we find the imagination takes over and the surrealist image is created. Within the image below (Figure 5.3) the child's drawing, created from their imagination, utilizes a range of known images already experienced to create a new imaginary vehicle, with the potential to take flight.

Encouraging children to use their imagination has to be developed and supported, in similar ways to that of other skills. Firstly, as mentioned below, the imagination needs to be fuelled by being exposed to a wealth of experience and images to draw upon. These experiences should be woven into the classroom art activities. The

Figure 5.3 Imaginative drawing

stimulus for the imagination can be found everywhere and the limitations are only confined to issues of age appropriateness. Exploring the outside environment, listening to music or examining a piece of artwork, can all be used to stimulate a child's imagination. Then, for the child to use their imagination they have to understand the possibilities that exist, to know that freedom exists, and have the self-confidence to support risk-taking in their work. Robinson (1995) suggests that all artwork involves elements of imagination, something that, on first consideration, we may find a challenging concept. For example, the child completing an observational drawing of a daffodil, having closely observed it as well as having been guided by the teacher, focuses constantly on drawing the flower, which one might otherwise consider as a task requiring limited imagination. However, Robinson (1995) suggests the imagination *is* used in drawing, for example in the inventive way that the child uses and combines materials to create the colour tone or texture of the daffodil. Without the child's perceived freedom in the teaching of the observation, the imagination cannot drive the process. It is often through observation that our imagination can be ignited, and the child's inventive exploration and expression takes hold.

Observation

The skill of observing is not only relevant to the subject of Art and Design, although the National Curriculum (DfE, 2013) clearly expects children to record their observations within it. The importance of observation is also key, for example, within the field of science. Ward and Roden (2016) suggested observation as a process skill within science and highlighted the importance of close observation to understand the details of objects or properties of the material. Although the purpose of observation may differ between art and science, the common skills can be taught across the curriculum. As the skill of observation can be challenging for children, the teacher needs to support the process through engaging them with interesting objects to observe and handle in art, just as in science (Edwards, 2013). When drawing or painting from observation, the process of seeing the object can be difficult for some children and may require the teacher to scaffold and deliberately support the act of observation. Through asking the child questions about the object, related to areas such as form, colour and tone, these can support the scaffolding of the child's observation and thus develop the drawing or painting. When drawing a still-life object such as a shell, the child observes the overall shape and may need support to observing the relationship with the surface the shell is sitting on, or the form or pattern of the shell. (See Figure 5.4.)

Observation can be focused around the visual and tactile elements of art, identified as *colour, pattern, texture, line, tone, shape, form* and *space* (Cox and Watts, 2007: 3). Using such prompts as areas to observe helps the child to look afresh, enhancing their observations by addressing these different elements. When making observations, it is important children are encouraged to make focused and repeated observations, either as a series of recordings of the same still-life object or as a continued study. Supporting children in these observations is vital and can lead to the creation of images with greater and more realistic understanding. 'Austin's Butterfly' (Berger, 2016) demonstrates how repeated observation and structured feedback can lead to drawings with greater detail and much closer representation of the observed object. This highlights two important points: firstly, the repeated observation ensures the child builds an understanding of the object, and, secondly, following this with a scaffolding approached for children where feedback allows for improvements within the process. With 'Austin's Butterfly', the feedback consisted of peers' comments about the observational drawing, which enabled Austin to refocus and re-engage with the drawing. There was no room for the erosion of confidence by ridicule or unpleasant comments. But this approach could have also been developed with different

Figure 5.4 Shell observational drawing

drawing activities or by utilizing a particular way of looking at the object such as through a viewfinder.

Why are the process skills important?

Quick pause moment – *Thinking more about the development of skills*:

- Consider which process skills you see being developed most often in school.
- How can we identify children's strengths within these skills?
- What skills do children need for future success?

The skills previously identified within this chapter are, initially, perhaps not those you might expect an Art and Design teacher to be concerned with. As a teacher, you might have identified the technical skills – for example the ability to shade with pastels or sculpt accurately with clay. However, the skills of invention, analysis, imagination, observation and expression are transferable life-enhancing skills (Robinson, 1989). These would then be identified not only within Art and Design but across all arts disciplines, and, for some elements, even within other subjects. The development of the child's ability with these skills will in turn support their development academically and in personal terms across their education (Eisner, 2002). If only taught the technical skills of materials a child can become proficient in such tasks but not in the creative processes. For example, a child could manipulate clay into an animal form successfully but if requested to create a fantastical beast without the skills of imagination, invention and analysis they would find the task extremely difficult if not impossible.

The beast within …

Here are some activities that illustrate how the teacher might approach a sequence of 'lessons' to encourage engagement with these process skills. They are based around the film/book *Fantastic Beasts and Where to Find Them* (Rowling, 2016), which is a continuation of her 'wizarding world' books. Although not identified as an example of fine art, the artistry evident during the process of creating the film is well worth our consideration. There were numerous creatures drawn and models made, along with computer-generated drawings. The main character, Newt Scamander arrives in

New York with an old brown leather suitcase, but something lies within. A small mischievous creature, which, on first viewing, one simply sees as long claws prising their way out of the old brown case …

Ask the children to consider the beast within, what might it look like? How big is it? What kind of nose does it have? What about other features? Inspire them with a clip or trailer of the film using questions such as these to stimulate thinking. Then children can begin to sketch their ideas in sketchbooks, with only a short five-minute response time before starting the drawing process. Allow some time to discuss their initial ideas with their peers and then give some further time to continue to draw, redraw and refine their initial idea. Once the drawing activity has been completed allow the children to start creating their beast using clay. Figures 5.5 and 5.6 show interpretations of the beast formed in clay, where children have collaboratively combined beastly elements from both drawings. It is important to stress at this point that children should have already been taught some clay skills, such as joining clay, using slip or making a figure self-supporting. Consider how long the children need to achieve success: all too often we rush children to get a piece finished. However, the activity could be further extended, for example creating an exhibition space for the creatures. Further consideration of the opportunities could easily develop this to become a cross-curricular lesson – the invented creature becoming the central figure in a range of activities, such as the creation of a habitat, or descriptive or imaginative writing.

This activity leads to opportunities to use both imagination and invention, while the technical skills required will develop and change throughout the child's life as materials, media and technologies change. These artistic skills enable individual children to develop their abilities and become creative thinkers (Fisher, 2005, 2013). The ability to develop children who have the capacity to become creative thinkers or imaginative inventors is essential for a successful society and economic growth.

Figures 5.5 and 5.6 Interpretations of the beast

(In fact, in 2016, the creative industries earned the United Kingdom approximately £10.5 million every hour – Creative Industries Federation, 2018.) These artistic skills should enable children to become creative individuals who impact on their own and the country's economic future success.

How does the teacher facilitate opportunities for autonomous learning/the child's autonomy?

Firstly, we might consider what this notion of autonomy might look like within Art and Design? If we are to understand what we are aiming to achieve, then success is more likely. When observing current practices within primary schools the notion of autonomy at times is distinctly lacking. Why is this the case? Partially this is due to the skills mentioned above not being recognized as key components within art, and this is then compounded by a pressured curriculum with so many outcomes to achieve.

Consider who selects the materials for a lesson. As teachers we should consider how accessible the resources are and whether children have choice in their selection of different materials. This is vital if we are to encourage children to make their own decisions and produce work that is individualized. This is not to mean that the teacher should allow the child free rein to use *any* resource, but there should be some opportunities for choice aimed at developing skills. For example, a choice could be offered when selecting drawing media: pencil, ink or charcoal; or the choice might be more constrained, depending on the objective, with a range of different pencils ranging from HB through to 6B, or various thicknesses, or perhaps a graphite stick instead of a pencil. Or the choice might be more expansive, with children selecting the technique to use, such as collage or painting, or selecting the size of the project. As the teacher, we need to enable the choice within the constraints of the objective and the task requirements. Having established the importance of choice of medias, we should also consider the accessibility of the resources to enable this freedom and an effective learning environment.

The actual organization of the materials also needs to be accessible for the child in order to encourage positive behaviours for learning. If children cannot see the resources, how are they aware that they can use them? Consider carefully who requires the resources and at what point in the lesson or day; if resources are organized into trays they can easily be moved from table to table or from side to desk, which would lead to reduced movement around the classroom by children. (This is of course, dependent on the space and classroom organization already established.) Consider these aspects of classroom organization: Does the activity take advantage of the space? Would a different layout be more supportive of the activity and the

Figure 5.7 A whole-school street carnival

ability for children to work autonomously? Consider the other spaces within the school as well, which of these might support the activity? (See Barnes, 2015.) Could working outside the classroom be more effective for the activity? (See Figure 5.7.)

The role of sketchbooks in supporting skills development

Engagement with sketchbooks is identified as a key requirement of practice within the National Curriculum for Art and Design for pupils in KS2 (DfE, 2013). Although using sketchbooks has been identified within previous curriculum documents, the current version of the National Curriculum has made this an explicit requirement. From our perspective there are too many schools that fail to comply with this require-ment (and, as already noted, the Office for Standards in Education, Children's Ser-vices and Skills (Ofsted) cannot see a reason why sketchbooks should not be used across the primary school age range – Ofsted, 2014).

As with all aspects of learning, children need to be taught how to be able to cre-ate sketchbooks that can become an effective record of their personal thinking and learning. This is not something that will just occur once a sketchbook is given to the child. The child needs to be taught to understand the value of their sketchbook. So, it is necessary to facilitate opportunities for children to explore, record, review and revisit their ideas. Sketchbooks are a place where skills of imagination, expression, invention and observation can be explored and developed. (See Figures 5.8 and 5.9.)

Figures 5.8 and 5.9 Observation and exploration within sketchbooks

Historically, artists, architects and designers from all walks of life have used a form of notebook to capture ideas and thought processes. Such books (or collections of papers) are a safe, personal place where ideas can be explored and refined. They provide a place to play with the imagination, record personal feelings and where skills and techniques can be practised (Adams, 2011). Using examples of artists' sketchbooks children can observe the practice of others to inform and develop their own. From Leonardo da Vinci to contemporary artists such as Grayson Perry (Perry, 2016), sketchbooks record the vision of the developing artist. Perry's sketchbooks (Perry, 2016) explores intermittent personal feelings and emotions reflecting many aspects of his life and the exploration of his sexuality. This use of a sketchbook in a personal and expressive nature is a more recent approach, as artists have developed the use of art to verbalize their feelings. The sketchbooks from artists such as Turner or Leonardo da Vinci lean more towards giving detailed life observations of their period in time. With da Vinci's sketchbooks one can observe the recordings of the human anatomy alongside images exploring his imagination such as imagery relating to flight (Wells, 2008). What is particularly apparent with Turner's, da Vinci's and Perry's sketchbooks is their personal nature – they clearly act as a tool for the artists to record their thinking, ideas and, importantly, curiosities. Children, as artists, are just as capable of using a sketchbook as a tool to process their thoughts (Hope, 2008), in much the same that artists have developed them over the years. This may not be the view shared with their teachers though.

Through the process of representing something from observation or imagination within the sketchbook, children are encouraged to engage in a deep reflection and critical consideration of the subject (Adams, 2011). A child's sketchbook can hold the explorations of their creative thinking, which, in turn, demonstrates to the observer their conceptual development and understanding. As each child's creative thinking and imagination differs, so therefore their sketchbooks should reflect this, becoming a private and personal space where the individual child can develop their own thoughts, interests and personal expression. The sketchbook can become the child's resource, a personal store of ideas, observations, curiosities and conceptual understanding, which the child can return to and develop at a later stage.

This said, Ofsted (2009) noted that pupils in KS2 (and also KS3) were not being encouraged to utilize a sketchbook in a similar way to artists and were thus missing out on a valuable learning resource to support their mastery of invention and imagination. Ofsted inspectors found that where Art and Design achievement was 'good' or better, effective sketchbooks were in use and that these books mirrored the way artists engage with their journals. Children's regular engagement with their own sketchbook also enabled them to develop ideas, explore a wide range of media, master valuable process skills, and critically reflect upon and evaluate their work (Ofsted, 2012). March's (2016) analysis of sketchbooks from primary classrooms found that schools often understood the potential positive outcomes of using sketchbooks but found creating opportunities for children to develop them as personalized journals within the curriculum was more challenging.

Several have identified that the way sketchbooks are used within primary classrooms varies considerably (Ofsted, 2009, 2012; March, 2016). The children's sketchbooks, if used to mirror the practice of a great artist, might contain observations, invention, exploration and imaginative images, alongside words and notes of explanation. These can then be seen as a tool to aid learning across the curriculum. As Robinson suggests, the sketchbook is 'a space or room where a child can think' to experiment and explore ideas or media (2011: 71). Children, as already noted, require support and guidance with the use of a sketchbook to enable them to understand the possibilities and develop the kinds of habits associated with a sketchbook (Allen, 2011). This requires the teacher to understand its personalized nature and the potential beyond the art lesson. When teachers understand and model this sketchbook process, children can begin to understand the potential and see it (as one pupil explained) like 'putting your brain on the page' (Toogood, 2004: 4).

How can teachers develop a good sketchbook habit?

How might the teacher instil and develop in the child the confidence to play within their sketchbook – whether it be with media, or concepts, or even words? As teachers there are activities that we can actively encourage to enable children to see the potential of the sketchbook to support and develop skills already discussed in this chapter. Adams (2003) says it is a tool that should have a regular place within the curriculum, not solely the domain of the art lesson, but a tool to support learning across the curriculum. The book becomes the record of the learning process, with activities reflecting all elements of the curriculum. Teachers should encourage drawing for a range of different purposes from observation, imagination, invention, expression, experimentation, interpretation, inspiration, fantasies, fascinations and fears (Adams, 2003).

Figures 5.10 and 5.11 An eight-year-old boy's robot drawings

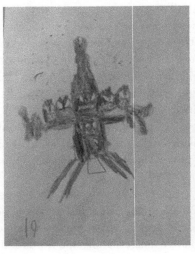

These drawings might occur in any number of lessons from an observation within science to an interpretation within history. The child might invent items, such as in the drawings above (see Figures 5.10 and 5.11) – this is an eight-year-old child's ideas relating to the creation of new robot, and here the child is focusing on form rather than the internal workings.

The sketchbook has become the place where the child plays with their imagination – using previously experienced images to build, extend and develop new ideas. As Robinson (1995, 2011) would advocate, the sketchbook is more than a place for the odd drawing within the art lesson, it is a place to think, a book where whoever is using it can develop their personal thoughts and interests to revisit at a later stage.

> When a sketchbook is treated as an experimental space for taking risks, trying things out, and learning through mistakes, it becomes a personal playground for ideas.
>
> (Robinson, 2011: 64)

This notion of play is key. Adams (2003) further suggests that the sketchbook should be seen as a source of fun and enjoyment that should not be overlooked. Education currently is preoccupied with academic outcomes, sometimes overlooking the pleasure and emotional engagement that is so key for developing well-being. A sketchbook can become an exciting space into which the child can dive – recording their thoughts, fears and emotions. The sketchbook can create a space to enable the user to play. The drawings below (in Figure 5.12) demonstrate how an eight-year-old girl used her sketchbook to play imaginatively, developing new characters, and using her previous observations and information to fuel her imagination. The use of a sketchbook in this way could support a child's creative writing development if utilized across the curriculum.

Figure 5.12 An eight-year-old girl's sketchbook

> ## Quick pause moment – *Thinking about the value of Art and Design in education*:
>
> - When did you last draw something?
> - Do you every find yourself doodling at times?
> - Most of us could draw before we could write, so how does drawing aid our written communication?

A good starting point for the sketchbook can be some simple drawing activities such as ones from observation. Ensure the objects are interesting and capture the child's attention, and consider how much freedom of choice there should be within the drawing process in relation to materials and time constraints. To ensure a personalized approach with the sketchbook, children need to feel they have the permission (from the teacher) and freedom to use the sketchbook beyond the constraints of the given activity or individual lesson. It is also a requirement in some schools that all staff keep their own sketchbooks, and the head teacher expects them to be brought to and used in staff meetings to clarify thinking and develop ideas.

So, thinking about your own school, are there opportunities within the school day for children to engage with their sketchbooks (if they wish) beyond the art lesson? Are children encouraged to experiment with media within their sketchbook, to question how charcoal might be affected if used in relation to ink, for example? How are watercolours used? How might watercolour paints be used to create an effective wash? The sketchbook becomes the place to explore and record all possibilities, a place where risks can occur and learning is visual (Toogood, 2004). It is also a place that is not always tidy or follows the same constraints or expectations as a maths or literacy book. The sketchbook records the starting points of ideas that may never be finished or reconsidered.

The form and style of the sketchbook should also be considered by the teacher: should they consist of a certain size, paper or quality of book? Or should there be freedom for children to create and make sketchbooks to suit their needs and preferences. The Access Art website (www.accessart.org.uk) has a number of simple ideas of how to make sketchbooks for any age. Sketchbooks can become more time limited to support and demonstrate thinking throughout a particular project. Equally they can have greater use over time to enable the child to reflect and consider previous learning. Both of these could be acceptable as long as children have the resources available to reflect on their previous creation(s). The sketchbook is a receptacle for the child's creative thinking, which can inform a number of pieces of work (Robinson, 2011), so this ability to reflect on previous books is also an important aspect.

How might we assess sketchbooks?

This is a challenging aspect as many of things previously outlined above considering the use of sketchbooks makes the assessment a challenge. If the sketchbook is to be a personal space for self-expression to think ideas through and record observations what elements should or could the teacher assess? As Robinson (2011) highlights, the sketchbook logs the learning journey, and it is this element that the teacher can assess through active conversations with the child about their work. We would not advocate marking against learning objectives, rather that they are used as opportunities for self- and peer-reflection of the sketchbook. Written comments by the teacher can be sensitively added, using, for example, a comment log at the back of the sketchbook or sticky notes (that can be removed at a later date by the child, should they wish). In some schools, the integrity of the sketchbook as the child's personal space means that the staff never record anything in (or on) the art it contains. Teachers can then question and encourage active thinking relating to elements within the sketchbook rather than, as we have observed on a number of occasions, highlighted learning objectives with limiting and banal comments such as 'nice picture' or 'good work' – which may have no real value without a longer conversation (see Chapter 7). These limiting assessments do not support skill development or creative thinking in relation to the contents of the sketchbook as there is no personal engagement in the interests or thoughts of the child. Teachers' comments that prompt analysis, invention or expression would have far greater value. These would enable the child to move forward in their creative development – as would comments that relate to specific technical skills (e.g. about the understanding of form or tone or the manipulation of a particular material).

Recommended reading

The following three texts are suggested as follow-on reading:

Adams, E. (2011), *Drawing It Makes You Think*. Hove: Drawing Power, The Big Campaign for Drawing.

March, C. (2016), *How Can the Sketchbook Support the Development of the Child's Thinking Skills?* Unpublished MA dissertation, University of Roehampton.

Robinson, G., Mountain, A. and Hulston, D. (2011), *Think Inside the Sketchbook*. London: Collins Education.

Chapter 6
Children's Ideas – Promoting Curiosity

Introduction

From the moment we arrive in the world, we are driven with a desire to know, learn, find out and discover. This powerful force is our innate ability to be curious. Curiosity is boundless and is something that, if allowed and encouraged, can sustain our hungry minds in an ongoing exploration throughout the course of our lives. Curiosity is a gift to both teacher and learner within all subjects and pedagogical paradigms as it motivates, intrigues and encourages investigation and knowledge. It is especially wonderful in art as it recognizes the child's instinct to open up and prod around at every opportunity, thus inviting new thinking and concepts in art.

This chapter will consider:

- What is curiosity?
- What does a curious child look like?
- How can curiosity be retained inside and outside the primary classroom through Art and Design?
- How is play important in curiosity and art?
- How do we share the process of curiosity and art as lifelong learners?

What is curiosity?

Curiosity – defined as 'a strong desire to know or learn something' (*Oxford Dictionaries*, 2011) – is the fuel that drives young minds to want to know more, the desire to get to the bottom of something and understand it more deeply. In citing early considerations of curiosity, Ostroff (2016) acknowledges curiosity as a driving force that brings learners to knowledge, keeping the flame of exploration alight in order to get to the answer. Curiosity is about being aware and open, checking things out, experimenting and interacting with one's surroundings. It is highly individualized, existing in a fused domain of emotion and cognition. Importantly the quenching of curiosity inevitably leads to added breadth and depth of knowledge (Peterson and Seligman, 2004).

Think, for a moment, about the last time you were curious. It might have been an item in a shop that caught your eye, or when you were on holiday and you just could not resist putting your toe in the water to try out the temperature. Moments like these are multitudinous in our daily lives. If we, as teachers, can tap into this innate pre-disposition and capture the imagination of our children, then we can maximize their interests and engagement. We all have this capacity to explore and investigate. It is, however, one of the most astounding and wonderfully fruitful attributes of childhood. Children's instinctive and overwhelming desire to find out and become immersed in curiosity-driven quests allows them to discover, think and refine (Tutchell, 2014).

What does a curious child look like?

A familiar sight to any teacher is the child who is involved and concentrating – jaw set and often with the tongue sticking out. Our concentrated adult expression equally takes on a certain characteristic of curious engagement. Contorted faces reveal the engaged absorption of a moment where something has caught our attention and drawn us in.

In his book about modern day curiosity, Ian Leslie proposes that;

> Curious people are more alive, somehow; their eyes are lit from behind.
>
> (Leslie, 2014: 14)

These moments of high involvement where curiosity is at the forefront will be prev-alent in any inspiring and creative classroom where children are 'looking curious'. Let us magnify and examine a curiosity-driven moment for a child. Try to consider a child and a moment when they absolutely *had* to explore and find out. Their eager-ness has a vigour, determination, and, importantly, an excited interest. There is no doubt that, in this moment, curiosity was the trigger for engagement and a conduit for learning in action. Curiosity motivates learning; a child is captured in a moment of wanting to know and so they are motivated to find out and consequently learn something new (Dowling, 2005). This busy and intensive cognitive laboratory devel-ops the ability to rationalize, realize and form opinions, as suggested in Figure 6.1.

Figure 6.1 The birth of curiosity (Tutchell, 2014: 12)

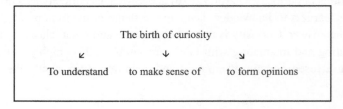

Curiosity vs. conformity

Curiosity is by nature subversive to the traditional, top-down classroom.

(Ostroff, 2016: 6)

The 'creative' climate in today's primary classrooms, as suggested in Chapter 1, is fighting to be heard and enjoyed as the pressure of the 'core' subjects remains contentiously omnipresent. The approach to education can, when conformity is constantly upheld, stultify the thrilling emotion and spontaneity of learning in pursuit of planning and precision, data and assessment.

For children to be able to express curiosity, they must feel able to ask and to seek, even if that means going against the grain and straying off at different tangents. To do this, we need to ensure and, in some cases, reinstate curiosity in our classrooms and schools, and so disengage the education system from standardization in both curriculum and assessment. The majority of our primary classrooms insist on tables and chairs arranged so that they take up the floor space of a room, which suggests that seated learning dominates. Curiosity-based learning is inherently dynamic and propulsive, not sedentary and passive (Shonstrom, 2014).

Thankfully there are schools that still manage to ensure creative learning is abundant in all subjects and yet at the same time to acknowledge the guidelines and rules laid out by government and inspection expectations. These are schools where Art and Design is still very much valued and celebrated. Such places offer themselves as creative laboratories of learning where the searching and discovery of answers and concepts is not linear but follows a path of excitement, individuality and curiosity.

There is no doubt that it is sometimes difficult to hold on to the values of curiosity in the classroom and of dynamic art teaching when the pressure of conforming to rules and regulations is a dominating force. It is especially difficult when new to the teaching profession. It is worth remembering, however, that the most important factor is teaching the children, not the data we churn out. Children, who are born curious and children whose curiosity is continually nurtured, make for a wonderfully dynamic, alive and knowledge-rich classroom. When provided with the freedom and scaffolding to pursue their own interests, they can and will become efficient, joyful super-learners (Gray, 2013). 'Good' results will continue to come out of this classroom to satisfy the league tables and data collectors, but, more importantly, teachers will create spaces where the most essential skills for deep learning are germinated – the curiosity and ideas classroom. Be brave and hold on to your values – remember why you decided to teach in the first place – it was *not* because of data and assessment.

Layers of enquiry

Behind every problem, solution or innovation lie questions and layers of enquiry.

(Patterson, 2015: 1)

Ideas come from being curious and wanting to find out. Curiosity can ignite a knock-on effect of learning, thus triggering layers of knowledge gathering. This strata-shaped paradigm gives important credence and full admission to find out and discover the 'what ifs' and the 'whys' in order to develop one's own artistic character and styles. New York-based artist, Sara Genn, maintains one of the essential stages of artistic endeavour is to 'make a searching and fearless inventory of your creative curiosity' (Genn, 2014).

Although most educators aspire to valuing and encouraging children's questions, this can cause discomfort, more often than not, in relation to time pressure or lack of subject knowledge. Both these barriers are surmountable – make more time, allow pause for thought and find time to discover the answer together. If we truly desire our children to become lifelong learners in art, we must acknowledge that the promotion of learning through questions is essential, and that children must have the opportunity not only to ask questions but also to enjoy a creative space to explore, discover and uncover their innate inquisitiveness. This thirst for information as we grow, mature and develop our understanding of the world encompasses curiosity as exploration. Benedict elaborates on this as 'the quest to penetrate forbidden areas and the ambition to go beyond' (Benedict, 2001: 254). The art classroom should be filled with children who are tingling with curiosity-led energy, ready to find out, discover and unpeel their layers of questions.

'Project-based learning' (Phillips, 2014; Ogier, 2017) is a creative teaching practice in which children are provoked by exposure to objects or experiences and then come up with problems and questions that drive their own learning. Such practice links to all subjects within the primary classroom but it is especially key to art where children enquire, research and investigate through practice activities and the handling of materials and art tools.

A culture that adopts this project-based and curiosity-driven pedagogy, inevitably means a classroom where the teacher is willing to take risks, allow for surprises and, importantly, instigate examples of exciting, challenging and daring projects that inspire, involve and provoke multiple questions.

Quick pause moment – *When was the last time that you* …:

- Created a mystery within the classroom space?
- Ask what happened next?
- Used a 'what if' in your teaching?
- Spiced-up your classroom?

Pandora's box

Much like the old story of 'Pandora's Box', the temptation to open up something unknown, the mystery of what is inside, and the unpredictability of the contents holds a risk. As Ostroff comments, curiosity is 'much like wildfire: it cannot be tamed, it will take sudden new turns or directions, and it will seek fuel in whatever way it can' (2016: 3). This dynamic can be a little unnerving for the teacher, as it means 'letting go' and allowing space for risk-taking, dynamic investigation and a strong sense of surprise. Although such learning encounters will be risky, dangerous and full of subversive possibilities, happily they will also be full of creative possibilities (Phillips, 2014). It ultimately means that we have to divest some of our learned control of a situation, which is not easy as this what we have become accustomed to doing. Taking risks and embracing surprise in Art and Design in the classroom leads to the most exciting and thought-provoking adventures, as Eisner's words describe:

> Surprise is one of the rewards of work in the arts. In addition, it is from surprise that we are most likely to learn something. What is then learned can become part of the individual's repertoire and once it is part of that repertoire, new and more complex problems can be generated and successfully addressed.
>
> (Eisner, 2002: 8)

Unlocking the unknown

Dowling (2005) refers to children's experiences of 'transcendence', where their great adventures and explorations of the unknown enable them to reach out to the limits of their world as part of growing up (Eglinton, 2003). The joy of spending time with children is that they can remind us of a beautiful spider's web that has droplets hanging from it, that the moon is out at the same time as the sun, or that there is a ladybird crawling up a brick wall. It is this innate sense of wonder that will lead and support our children's and students' lifelong journeys of discovery and learning – we want them to be, as Patterson and Roberts call it, 'agents of wonder' (2015: 1).

Spaces of curiosity

To ensure our children have continuous and plentiful opportunities to be agents and discover, explore and wonder, we need to re-examine and re-energize the spaces in which they learn. Small adaptations and considerations can transform a classroom into a container for an exciting new mode of learning – it becomes a space where the most essential skills for deep learning are germinated – it becomes the curiosity classroom (McFall, 2013). The classroom no longer exists as a sedentary base that ploughs through 'curriculum fodder' but rather becomes a space for curiosity (Phillips, 2014) where creativity, experimentation, learning and innovation are valued. So how do we realize, design and make real these spaces of curiosity with a particular emphasis on Art and Design in the primary classroom? It is worth remembering here, that when we refer to spaces indoors and outdoors are intertwined.

The unexplored art cupboard

Included in the 'unlocking process' is the mystery of the unexplored 'art cupboard', which contains a range of materials, depending on each school's budget for such things. It is can be a place of wonder for teachers themselves, as, hidden below the depths and often under a layer of dust, exist unexposed and unused materials. Such gems could instigate and enthral a whole class of children if they could be dusted off and given daylight. Art cupboards such as these are the 'Aladdin's caves' of curiosity, as they can give rise to huge amounts of curiosity if both teachers and children are allowed to investigate and explore their contents. Behind all this is the fact that materials, tools and equipment can stimulate children's discoveries in Art and Design and therefore engender a heightened wave of learning, which is further increased due to motivational curiosity. How does something work? What could I do with that piece of paper? If I combine these two colours, what will happen? The questions are endless and open, allowing both children and adults to take control and become masters and mistresses of curiosity in Art and Design learning and understanding.

Cabinets of curiosities

Throughout history, there are examples of 'spaces' of curiosity, such as the art cupboard and all it contains. The *Wunderkammer* or *Kunstkammer*, as they were originally called with reference to their German names, were cabinets of curiosity stemming back to the sixteenth century. They were spaces dedicated to encyclopaedic collections of objects, generally belonging to natural history, geology, ethnography, archaeology, religious or historical relics, works of art and antiquities.

> The Kunstkammer was regarded as a microcosm or theater of the world, and a memory theater. The Kunstkammer conveyed symbolically the patron's control of the world through its indoor, microscopic reproduction.
>
> (Fiorani, 1998: 268)

The common feature of 'spaces' such as wonder rooms, cabinets of curiosity or boxes of tricks is that they need to be opened in order to be discovered. We all know the sensations of that moment before opening something, whether it is a door, an envelope, a parcel, a birthday present – the sense of anticipation, the unknown, the curiosity about what is inside. (See Figure 6.2.) Discovering the contents is high on the agenda, with the following examples of practice and projects from around the world that have continued to enhance children's learning in Art and Design through a curiosity perspective.

Figure 6.2 Curiosity can be infectious: parents exploring children's artwork at their own exhibition

Agent of wonder

In one school in England, there exists a wonder room where its creator, 'agent of wonder' Matthew McFall, has filled a small space with an exotic plethora of objects, artefacts and odds and ends. The contents are then studied, considered, questioned and pored over by the children at the school. This has led to an abundance of imagination in their artwork, creative writing and their ability to ask questions and ponder causes and reasons. Arnott (2011) states, in recognition of McFall's inspirational practice, that *research* suggests that providing hands-on experiences raises questions, answers some, then raises more among inquiring young minds. 'Real curiosity doesn't fit into neat 50 minute chunks … it nags and eats and provokes long after the bell at the end of a lesson.'
(Source: https://www.theguardian.com/education/2011/may/31/wonder-room-nottingh am-university-academy.)

Room 13

The story of Room 13 began in 1994, when a group of children established their own art studio in Room 13, Caol Primary School, near Fort William, Scotland.

This ingenious, inspirational and child-led initiative has continued to thrive over the last twenty-four years, and its impact internationally has been astounding as Room 13 has gone on to establish a network of creative studios and a thriving community of young artists and entrepreneurial thinkers that stretches across the globe.

In most cases, schools and children have appropriated spaces that operate in a similar way to the very first Room 13. The children create ownership of the space; they work with an artist (teacher or resident) to help inspire projects and ideas; and they join their ideas and gallery images with other Room 13s from around the world. It is a continually evolving and hugely innovative project that inspires hundreds and thousands of children and adults alike. At the heart of all these Room 13s is the freedom and encouragement to open up curious minds in art and try out ideas and projects.

> Art produced with confidence and integrity by young artists in Room 13 encapsulates an expression of their own experiences, curiosities, and worldview ... the creativity and critical thinking skills demanded in the studio environment foster a confidence that will enable them to lead the way in exploring new applications of these tools that will be necessary as they grow or find their place in the workplaces of the future.
>
> (Gibb, 2012: 243)

Reggio Emilia and the Remida recycling centre

The Italian Reggio Emilia preschools are renowned internationally for their highly creative and child-initiated education systems. The approach to Art and Design in these inspirational schools makes them role models for excellent practice in learning and understanding in creative and expressive media and this pedagogy is easily transferable to the older years of schooling.

> The approach is established within a pedagogy of both scientific and artistic enquiry, which values children's personal responses to self-initiated lines of investigation.
>
> (Ogier, 2017: 12)

In conjunction with the art-based practice that is sustained within the schools, there also exists a space that houses a wealth of creative possibilities – a recycling centre called Remida. It was established in 1996 in Reggio Emilia and is a cultural project focused on sustainability and research on creativity and waste materials. It fosters the idea that waste materials, in their imperfect state are able to stir artistic ideas and reflections, thus avoiding the definition of 'useless' and 'waste'. The materials of

Remida are supplied by approximately 200 companies that deliver wastage, defective materials or production surplus destined for disposal, which the centre recovers and proposes as subjects to investigate.

The centre is visited every year by more than 3,000 teachers, artists, students, children and interested people from all over the world. Curiosity is at the core of this centre's appeal and fascination – a curiosity to touch, prod, open, extract, pull apart and reconstruct in creative and energetic ways. One visitor describes it as 'a place to dwell where objects, with their own charm and history, open boundless worlds of unexpected surprises, unusual forms' (Gualtieri, 2018).

The 'Drawing Room'

Hannah Yason is an artist and educator who works with children of all ages, especially those who experience emotional and behavioural difficulties. For one particular project, she created four drawing boxes, which were designed as safe, enclosed and personal spaces for children, one at a time, to enter and become immersed in the private and creative space, called a 'Drawing Room'. This project was created for a township school in Cape Town, South Africa. (See Figures 6.3–6.5.)

Figures 6.3, 6.4 and 6.5 The 'Drawing Room' in action

In Hannah words:

I wanted to connect with the underprivileged children who go to school in a township literally in the middle of gang violence. They are constantly in danger and their school is extremely under-funded and lacking in resources etc.

In each of the Drawing Rooms was a container of tools and drawing materials. The idea was to create ripe conditions for play and self-expression. Ink, pastels, charcoal and paint were selected as the most fluid and spontaneous materials with a felt-tip for the familiarity value. Although a brush as available, so too was a sponge and pipette which enabled a non-precious approach to the process.

Once inside, most children hesitated at first and many did not know what some of the materials and tools were, after an explanation they slowly engaged. It was a moving experience to see the children own the space inside and most fell naturally into a deep silence, focussing on their own use of the materials and tools.

(Hannah Yason in *AD Magazine*, 2015: 32)

The following two examples outline 'curiosity-based' projects in existence, which are highly accessible as examples and can easily be mirrored and adapted in any classroom or school.

The wonderwall

The concept of a large vertical surface, which offers a space for interaction, mark-making and collaborative responses on a regular and ad hoc basis, enhances a questioning culture. All respondents, both children and adults, suggest, draw, write, post an image whenever and however the moment takes them. Some questions are given answers by others, some images are added to, some post-ups are reciprocated in a visual response. It is a 'living wall', which continues to thrive and breathe thanks to its creators – an ongoing vertical and image-filled journal that documents the thoughts, questions and curious minds of its interlocutors. It offers up a space where learning and affect are inextricably entwined, moving between feelings of excitement and curiosity to accomplishment and satisfaction.

Sketchbook circle: student teachers

Taking ideas from the inspiring 'Sketchbook circle' project (Brass and Coles, 2014) in which teachers swap sketchbooks regularly with a partner and add their own work to or on the existing pages, a group of first-year teacher education university students

Figure 6.6 Sketchbook circle books

set off on a collaborative path of ongoing discovery. They each collated a sketchbook and a theme of joint interest was agreed. On the first occasion, the theme was 'rubbish' – an interesting choice, and one that possibly related to the excess of freshers' week! The fourteen members of the group each took a slip of paper from the book of names and away they went with their sketchbooks in hand and the name secretly stowed away. (See Figure 6.6.)

Three days later, the students gathered, and the sketchbooks were brought in but were kept unopened. Names were selected once again, and the books were passed on to that new receiver. The page to be completed responded to the preceding sketchbook entry. The students continued to perform this secret exchange over the first term. After eleven weeks, the sketchbooks were returned to their original owners and the contents fully revealed. This unveiling moment naturally engendered a lively buzz of excitement and anticipation with a great amount of noise and enjoyment as the illustrated pages opened up. That flame of curiosity within this simple sketchbook circle project then cascaded into their own teaching practices resulting in some inspirational class-based artwork.

The great outdoors – art without a ceiling

An outside art space is open – the fresh air, the exposure to the weather of the day, the lack of walls and the infinite expanse of the sky above can increase an exuberance of activity within a human body. A child can experience a particular freedom of expression and engagement, which is often absent in an inside space with walls and a ceiling. The mystery of outside space and its infinite layers of landscape offer the curious mind a chance to develop the tactile and haptic knowledge of the world in a way that a closed classroom does not always encourage (McWilliams, 2008).

There are outside spaces that lend themselves very easily to the curious mind, spaces that offer hidden corners, shaded dells, complex branch-laid dens and dense leaves to forage in. The woods are great spaces of encounter (Hawkins, 2011) for art and particularly for natural art, where objects of interest can be slightly hidden from view, so that curiosity has to be used to discover their delights and contents. The elemental qualities of space, air, weather and size all create an area where the freedom to play with art is often on a larger and messier scale. It is less confined, less rule-based and often more collaborative. The weather and climate can make these curiosity-driven experiences temporary and transitional – another inspiring and motivational qualification.

Sites such as the Forest of Dean Sculpture Trail offer art appreciation adventures that encourage a sensory response within the disposition of curiosity. The beautiful outdoor spaces of hidden dips and majestic trees allow a wonderfully tactile relationship between artist and geographical space. Moments such as these are described by Hawkins (2011) as 'dialogic moments between artist, site and community' (Hawkins, 2011: 471). They offer creative possibilities relating to the dynamic processes of place and landscape, and the art they can promote owing to the tactile nature and multidimensional quality of the great outdoors and flora and fauna (Rogoff, 2000). As the weather changes and the natural environment makes its seasonal adaptations, so the sculptures and art pieces naturally change their appearance due to light, rain, sun, snow, shadows and anything else the natural world throws their way.

In the following examples, the spaces, activities, initiatives and projects are again, as before, transferable to primary teaching practice.

Layers in the landscape

These reshape learners' worlds by enabling them to go beyond just photographs, providing encounters where they can discover their own way of seeing and experiencing a landscape (Tutchell and Witt, 2015). Layering small landscaped vignettes within outdoor spaces using boxes, drawings, transparent designs (as above) offers an awareness of the qualities of Art and Design leading them to look for, recognize and appreciate beauty in urban and rural landscapes. (See Figures 6.7–6.9.)

Figures 6.7, 6.8 and 6.9 Layers in the landscape

Figure 6.10 Colours in ice

Ink snow and ice

Squeeze or pipette coloured ink or food colour onto snow or icy puddles and watch. The colours will merge in the snow and run through cracks in the ice to create coloured rivulets. Control over what happens is limited but fascinating! (See Figures 6.10 and 6.11.)

Figure 6.11 Colours left after a week of melting snow

Spray textiles – colour stained grass/tarmac

Use plant misters to spray coloured water onto lengths of paper or fabric laid over an outside surface. The spray will leave an extended trail of marks beyond the edge of the paper or fabric and will also leave a stained and interesting residue when lifted off.

Big charcoal rubbings

Long and wide lengths of varied paper pieces can be used to rub textures of trees and bark, walls and ground surfaces. Paper can be wrapped around the width of trees or scale long meandering walls. Individual pieces can join up to create a long line of textured explorations to be walked along, surveyed and compared. The dense velvety quality of the charcoal and its material sympathy with the exterior textures will be experienced.

Sky photography

Trajectorial tendencies cause young children to look up – a lot of the world they exist in is higher than them and so they spend much of their time looking up to

Figure 6.12 Sky photography in action

things. This includes the sky and its ever-changing landscape of colours, clouds and movement. Photography, video clips and bird's-eye view chalk and pastel sketches record this altering and transitional arena that surrounds us. Capturing daily pictures affords young children a sense of something that is vast, intangible and mighty. (See Figure 6.12.)

Speed date chalk-a-thon

An aisle of two lines of children can be formed along a paved or tarmac space. Using chalks, make marks in response to a chosen theme for one minute at a time, so that facing partners work together creating an image in response to one another – mirroring each other's movements and meeting in the middle section of their pavement. When the minute is up, move along and meet the next facing partner – a lively, animated and collaborative chalked frieze will begin to emerge. (See Figure 6.13.)

Figure 6.13 Speed date chalk-a-thon in progress

Wonder hole

With a timetable heavily biased towards the core subjects – an all too familiar scenario in our current KS2 classes – one young, lively and adventurous newly qualified
teacher decided to incentivize his Year 5 class who felt a little 'chained to their desks'.
He introduced a 'wonder hole' during the weeks leading up to SATs when all felt a
little gloomy and the grey days were ongoing. At some point in the day, whenever it
felt most conducive, the class would venture outside to the school grounds to a hole
created by the teacher. He had found a discrete spot that only his class and he knew
about (as far as the children were concerned). They would take it in turns to see what
had been hidden in this spot and so reveal a mystery on a daily basis. The tradition of
walking to the hole, digging it up and unveiling the contents became a much-waited-
for moment. Such was the status of being the 'digger-upper', that the children were
delighted when it was their turn. The contents would then be used somehow during
the school day, whether it was to incentivize creative writing, be used as an artefact of
historical enquiry, scientific discovery or a mathematical equation. This very simple

daily adventure fed in to every discipline and mode of learning, tapping into a very motivational and yet highly accessible human disposition – curiosity.

'Mud between your toes'

This programme was launched over ten years ago in early years settings, providing young children with a space in which to be noisy, physical and exuberant, and giving them the freedom to be inquisitive, adventurous, innovative, creative and messy (Phillips, 2014). By encouraging both teachers and children to reconnect children with the outside world, play and sculpture-building with natural materials were all created by the children in bare feet – literally 'mud between the toes'. A fully sensory experience was had by all who participated, and a lot of very messy footprints entertained the school grounds as a consequence – an installation in itself.

> ### Quick pause moment – *Thinking about making Art and Design in education*:
> - When did you last use the outside space available to you for an art activity?
> - Have you gone out and created artworks in all weathers, making the most of the elements and their transformative effect?
> - When you are outside with your children for an art project, how do you observe the difference in their learning dispositions to when they are inside?
> - Which of the examples given above might excite curiosity for your class? (Or you and your colleagues?)

Curiosity-based art play

The activities, adventures and initiatives described previously can only really emerge, develop and evolve if we ensure that we include the very important 'play' factor in our children's art experiences. It would be very hard to experience that sense of curiosity combined with art if one were prevented from playing, as the physical need and moment of revealing and discovering comes from the human condition of playing and experimenting with things, not necessarily knowing what will happen and so playing with a mind open to discovery. That playing moment in art and curiosity is transformative in its experience and can often be a chaotic moment rather than a linear experience. Eisner refers to these early 'magnetic' explorations as 'micro-discoveries' (2002: 78). Discoveries are uncovered and also, very importantly, contain an element of surprise, as previously mentioned.

> Within us all there exists a powerful tug-of-war between a desire to satisfy curiosity, explore the unknown and a need to adhere to that which is familiar, comfortable and safe. For an artist, the challenge of the new, the magnetism of the unfamiliar, is stronger than the need to reinforce the status quo.
>
> (Prentice, 1995: 127)

Playing with art is not simply confined to the realms of childhood, it is something we all do, and artists often refer to this in their work. The artist Paul Klee once said: 'A line is a dot that went for a walk' (cited in Klee, 1960). As the dot is animated by the drawer's playful actions, it starts to transform into something. These very transformations are the conduit for artistic development and discovery. As one 'thing' becomes 'another', a very important process has taken place and play was the conduit.

Play in art allows for opportunities to find out and explore, and not only to do and finish. Paintings are often produced on a prolific scale in early years settings. These paintings are often created on a vertical easel, put on a drying rack and then either taken home or put away somewhere. Of course, there is no denying, the home-taking element is of high importance in the child's ownership stakes. And home-taking ensures artwork is shared with the family and further links are made between home and school. However, the proliferation is far more a consequence of the process-driven playing than it is of the end product.

This kind of play is an action that has no defined end, it is something that happens when we want to explore. Purpose, however, can still be very apparent as the child embarks on a playful journey that may be, perhaps, to do with curiosity about a particular material in the art area. The embarkation and continuation of play is an inquiry actively defined by the child. He or she is not passively reflecting a given reality or following a set of rules and a prescribed pattern of events.

> Hands-on inquiry properly redistributes the responsibility of learning to students, … the role changes from a passive recipient of information to a constructivist participant in the creation of understanding.
>
> (Zion, 2005: 876)

Individually owned curiosity entices children and causes physical actions of enquiry that belong, in their entirety, to them. The enquiry will always have some sort of purpose; otherwise it would not have happened in the first place. But that purpose need not be finite, and so the play continues. Here we can see the important stratification of art play – ideas and understandings assembling and coagulating. These strata, rich in creative knowledge, allow the children to use their play experiences as firm foundations for understanding themselves as artists. Cox (2005: 117) refers to this work in progress, this continued enquiry, as a young child's 'central source of data'.

Sharing the process

The more time you spend with children, the more you
Notice how inquisitive they are about the world and
How keen is their thinking even about the most subtle
Things – things which escape materiality, easy
Recognition, definite forms, and the laws of invariance,
Things you can touch but can't touch, that brush
Against the real and the imaginary, that have something
Of the mysterious about them and offer wide margins
Of interpretation.

(Loris Malaguzzi, cited in Strong-Wilson and Ellis, 2007: 43)

By sharing the art adventures experienced by children, we become part of them, and this ensures that the children's responses and engagement is at the forefront rather than imposing our own adult-based persuasions. Riding the wave with children (Tutchell, 2014) in art-making, encourages both the child and the adult to engage in a respected union of interest. Their responses to art-making can be discussed, considered and employed, but all within a constructively mutual and trusting arena.

Although in our work we can plan and provide some excellent tools, resources and spaces, we can never be sure what the curious young mind will find out. Quite often when we observe a child's moment of absorbed exploration and are comfortably assessing what is being played out and surmising their route of learning, the enquiry will follow something very different and go off on an alternative tangent that would have been impossible to predict.

We know that it is crucial for the child to be in charge of and in possession of their own endeavours, in order to define and progress their own artistic prowess and character. We also know how important it is for us to understand and embrace this ownership so that we value each new discovery and unravelling strand of curious engagement.

This is where our role as teachers of art becomes so important – our role as *co*-inquirers, *co*-researchers and *co*-curiositas! Co-creating a curiosity classroom requires some degree of humility. We have to cease being in charge and listen to the multitude of voices in the classroom with equal respect (Ostroff, 2016). Supporting curious children is best achieved when teachers themselves are curious, when they are excited, involved, self-directed and trying new things.

Such a teaching style demands a high level of engagement and energy: filling the many roles of motivator, diagnostician, guide, innovator, experimenter, researcher, modeller, mentor and collaborator (Crawford, 2000). What it promises, however, and why it is all worth it, is, in Phillips' words:

Spaces in which the spirit of adventure thrives.

(Phillips, 2014: 495)

Astounding artists – lifelong learning

Broadhead (2004) refers to children as 'astounding'. They are indeed this in their ability to capture the moment and make connections fast and furiously. They are also astounded by the world itself and when we can recognize this, as practitioners, we too can participate and experience their engagement. We can never be children again, in the true sense of the word, but we can enjoy, relish and recognize the experiences of wonder through them. If we reaffirm this in our thoughts and actions, as the following reminders indicate, we remember why we wanted to work with them in the first place.

Quick pause moment – *When was the last time you*:

- Looked at things with children?
- Valued the moments when children stop and stare?
- Took time to watch and observe children's absorbed attention?
- Watched children's gestures?
- Listened, really listened, to children's words?
- Gave children time to look and ponder?

This checklist of experiences reminds us of how important curiosity is in its ability to supercharge learning. It is something that continues throughout our lives. It is a lifelong learning tool. Psychologists view curiosity as a life force, vital to happiness, intellectual growth and well-being. Co-creating adventures in art with a classroom of children ensures this lively and inspiring experience will continue on a regular basis.

Conclusion: Googling curiosity – a 'hollow' experience

Everything is easy to figure out by Googling it; we never get to prolong the heady rush of curiosity.

(Shonstrom, 2014: 2)

Our final word of this chapter is a reminder about what long and sustained curiosity is *not*. The temptation to google for an answer is all too common. This is not so terrible if done occasionally but what it does not do is delve down deep and quench curiosity in its rightful place. We sometimes confuse the practice of curiosity with the ease of access to information and forget that real curiosity requires the exercise of effort (Leslie, 2014). The Googling model focuses on the goals of learning rather than valuing learning for itself. In other words, developing the rich experience of epistemic curiosity – states of mind that have been aroused by novel questions, complex ideas, ambiguous statements and unsolved problems (Litman, 2005).

The immediacy of the Googled answer makes it all too easy and, often, fairly superficial – the answer is there, no effort, no ruminating, just offered straight up. As Leslie (2014) affirms;

> Epistemic curiosity is hard work; it involves sustained cognitive effort. That makes it tougher, but ultimately more rewarding.

> (Leslie, 2014: 35–6)

In order to achieve what Leslie advocates, teachers must strive to create learning environments that stimulate a deeper and more satisfying knowledge. We must continually remind ourselves of how powerful curiosity is as a learning tool and its ability to:

- feed the mind and the imagination;
- serve as a human search engine;
- ignite research;
- stimulate discovery trails;
- be endless; and
- find meanings and rationale.

Recommended reading

The following four texts are suggested as follow-on reading:

Adams, J.N., Worwood, K., Atkinson, D., Dash, P., Herne, S. and Page, T. (2008), *Teaching Through Contemporary Art: A Report on Innovative Practices in the Classroom*. London: Tate Publishing.

Adams, E., (2003), *Power Drawing Notebooks*. Hove: Drawing Power, The Big Campaign for Drawing.

Wilson, T. (2005), *Art and Design in Suffolk: Key Stages 1 and 2*. Ipswich: Suffolk County Council.

Wilson, T. (2007), *Art in the Early Years*. Ipswich: Suffolk County Council.

Chapter 7
Assessing Children in Art and Design

Introduction

The majority of primary school teachers in England seem to have a tendency to think one of two things about assessing children's Art and Design work: either it is too difficult because of the subjectivity of the subject as a whole, or it is somehow wrong for adults to attempt to do so as it will label or otherwise negatively affect the maker of the work. Neither of these is a helpful starting point for us but we should deal with the essence of the arguments lest readers conclude that we hold such beliefs.

In this chapter, we will consider these topics:

- The possibility of assessment in Art and Design
- Why assess children's learning in Art and Design?
- What could be assessed in Art and Design?
- Assessing children beyond levels in Art and Design
- What does assessment actually look like in primary Art and Design?
- Planning for progression
- What about the inspectors' view?
- Further help and support

The possibility of assessment in Art and Design

There may be some truth in the arguments above as art forms can spark very different responses from the viewer. Depending on one's point of view, some of the great artists of the past can either be dismissed as 'unphotographic' (for example, most Impressionist painters, Picasso, Braque or van Gogh) or highly admired because of their ability to capture 'a true likeness' (for example, any of the Dutch great masters, Escher or Dali) – or perhaps the very contrary! As we have already noted, this argument can indicate a narrowness of interpretation by the viewer, and when the viewer is empowered, as in the role of a teacher, potential harm can be inflicted on whole classes of children. As teachers, the basis of our assessment must be more than just what we like or dislike. This is crucially important, as too many teachers have used such criteria in order to make their own judgements or (worse still) persuade their colleagues to also adopt them across the whole-school community. Let's move on to consider the second objection before returning to consider in some detail what and how we ought to be assessing children's Art and Design work.

The position whereby adults do not believe they can make any judgement about the pupils' work is equally problematic. We feel that there is no other area of the curriculum where this view is as common as in Art and Design. The reason for this is really a lack of understanding by the teachers themselves. If only they had an idea of what 'good art' is as well as a depth of understanding of how children develop in their ability to see, represent and record their world (whether real or imagined), then teachers would find it impossible to think in this way. What is clearly true is that teachers do wield considerable power. The way we respond, act, comment or remain silent can be powerful tools in moulding or affecting the ways in which the child may go on to create in the future. How many student teachers have we heard tell instances from their own childhood that convinced them that they 'couldn't do art'? These stories reveal depths of feelings that affect people for decades, usually stemming from when a teacher has convinced, or sometimes confused, a pupil to think that what they have produced was of such poor quality that they ought to give up trying. The confusion sometimes has arisen when a teacher has praised another piece of work or compared the work from several pupils only to demoralize the previously enthusiastic learner. The desire to protect future pupils from such emotional pain is often the reason that teachers conclude that they shouldn't make judgements about the artwork children produce in their classrooms. Unsurprisingly, we cannot agree with this view: we must develop the confidence in teachers to enable them to make assessments and we must develop inner confidence within the students.

The consequence of both these thought paths is the weakening of the subject across the curriculum and also in the minds of the learning community. In this chapter, we want to strongly focus on why assessment should be regarded as key, what should actually be assessed, and, to some extent, how this might be achieved. (We recognize there could be some variation on the last point depending on the agreement reached in the particular context of the schools or communities of schools where the reader is based.)

Quick pause moment – *What do you think at this point?*

- How much has your past experience affected your view of assessment in Art and Design?
- Are you already questioning the practice (or the lack of practice) that you see around you?
- Can you recognize the factors we've mentioned so far?

Why assess children's learning in Art and Design?

Assessment itself needs some careful reflection. It is part of the process by which all parties (pupils, teachers and parents) can explain and understand the steps made in learning. For teachers, this process involves the ongoing, continuous activity of observing pupils, talking together with them, noting issues and informing the planning of the next stages of development. This is known as formative or assessment for learning. The best teachers develop a range of strategies involving question construction (see Jennings, 2006; Gregory, 2015) or ways of noting and recording their dialogue or observations. Much of this rich, experience-led observation activity will be missed by adults who rush the art lesson and who do not take time and care to extend their own strategies. Tutchell (2014) explores the ways in which this can be done successfully in the classroom. She considers the process from a number of viewpoints – including the aspects of narratives that link with the production of images, the reflection of the physical use of the body as well as verbal language and 'silent and energised concentration' (Tutchell, 2014: 86). We would recommend her work for further reading and reflection.

Related to this ongoing form of assessment is summative assessment – more commonly associated with SATs in core subjects or end-of-unit tests. Some readers might be surprised to learn that such tests do exist for Art and Design (see Qualifications and Curriculum Authority (QCA), 2006). Teachers have often discounted them as being less than helpful in building the bigger picture of pupils' progress in the subject. For the children themselves, forms of assessment might include self-assessment (or evaluation) or peer-assessment – but both rely on the teacher (leading the introduction of such activities) having a clear understanding of the purposes and opportunities that these forms provide, as well as the implicit challenges that they may pose in the busy classroom. These activities also require an acknowledgement of the importance of giving respect to even young pupils' views (Meager, 2012). In fact, the importance of listening to the views of children about their own artwork is frequently overlooked (Bowden, Ogier and Gregory, 2013). The parental view of assessment will to a large extent either reflect their own levels of understanding of the subject and/or the information conveyed by the school over time. Some will not be satisfied with an annual report of two or three lines whereas others will feel that this is all that the subject demands. Arts Council England (ACE, 2016) has produced some guidance for school governors and trustees that could better support the reporting to parents by posing challenging questions about the intentions and provisions made in the school.

In the coming pages, we will explore most of these assessment forms.

What could be assessed in Art and Design?

We feel strongly that assessment ought to take account of all aspects of pupils' learning and achievement – not only what is produced but also how it was produced, the skills acquired as well as the knowledge of the tools and materials used (China and Gast, 2014). This might seem to pose a big challenge for teachers, but those who aim for mastery themselves will appreciate that it stems from the depth of understanding that they are able to build upon as well as use effectively. China and Gast (2014) suggest that there are four progress objectives to be understood and then woven into the assessment process:

- **Generating ideas**: the skills of designing and developing ideas;
- **Making**: the skills of making art, craft and design;
- **Evaluating**: the skills of judgement and evaluation; and
- **Knowledge**: both technical process and cultural context.

These objectives can also be presented in a helpful diagrammatic form to aid the conceptualization of what might be assessed (see Figure 7.1).

The question as to why to assess Art and Design lies beneath this conceptual map: it ought to aid the development of understanding of the teacher so that they can more specifically focus their teaching as well as the communication with others (both pupils and their parents) about the learning journey undertaken thus far and pointing towards the future pathways. This becomes clearer in their suggested outlines for how these might be expanded and used with a class-based recording mark sheet (see Table 7.1).

Figure 7.1 Four progress objectives

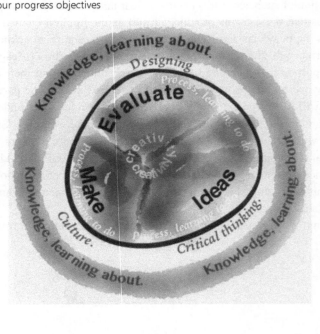

Table 7.1 Suggested expansion of early years and KS1 progress objectives

Skills	EYFS By the end of the EYFS pupils should be able to	Year 1 By the end of Year 1 pupils should be able to:	Year 2 By the end of Year 2 pupils should be able to
Generating ideas *Skills of designing and developing ideas*	1. work purposefully responding to colours, shapes, materials, etc. 2. create simple representations of people and other things	1. recognize that ideas can be expressed in artwork 2. experiment with an open mind *(for instance, they enthusiastically try out and use all materials that are presented to them)*	1. try out different activities and make sensible choices about what to do next 2. use drawing to record ideas and experiences
Making *Skills of making art, craft and design*	3. work spontaneously and enjoy the act of making/creating 4. sustain concentration and control when experimenting with tools and materials	3. try out a range of materials and processes and recognize that they have different qualities 4. use materials purposefully to achieve particular characteristics or qualities	3. deliberately choose to use particular techniques for a given purpose 4. develop and exercise some care and control over the range of materials they use *(for instance, they do not accept their first mark but seek to refine and improve)*
Evaluating *Skills of judgement and evaluation*	5. recognize and describe key features of their own and others' work	5. show interest in and describe what they think about the work of others	5. When looking at creative work express clear preferences and give some reasons for these *(for instance, be able to say 'I like that because ...')*
	By the end of the EYFS pupils should know:	By the end of Year 1 pupils should know:	By the end of Year 2 pupils should know:

(Continued)

Table 7.1 (Continued)

	EYFS	Year 1	Year 2
Skills	By the end of the EYFS pupils should be able to	By the end of Year 1 pupils should be able to:	By the end of Year 2 pupils should be able to:
Knowledge and under-standing *Acquiring and applying knowledge to inform progress*	6. that art, (design and craft) is made by artists exhibiting care and skill and is valued for its qualities 7. how to explain what they are doing	6. how to recognize and describe some simple characteristics of different kinds of art, craft and design 7. the names of the tools, techniques and the formal elements (colours, shapes, tones, etc.) that they use	6. that different forms of creative works are made by artists, craft-makers and designers, from all cultures and times 7. and be able to talk about the materials, techniques and processes they have used, using an appropriate vocabulary *(for instance, they know the names of the tools and colours they use)*

Source: China and Gast, 2014: 7, reproduced with permission

In order to capture the progress of each class, the recording format could be set out using a simple colour coding to indicate the teacher's assessment against these progress objectives for each unit studied. (Green for exceeding expectations, orange for meeting and red for not yet meeting them.)

Generating ideas: skills of designing and developing ideas

Another perspective for development is for pupil self-evaluation. Jennings (2006) offers some suggestions for statement banks for KS2 pupils to complete themselves over the year in order to aid their self-evaluation and build a picture of their view of progress they have made.

- I know that ideas can be expressed in pictures and objects.
- I can experiment with an open mind (for instance, I am keen to try out and use all materials that my teachers put out for the class to use; I don't just use things I know or think will work best).
- I try out lots of different art activities and make sensible choices about what to do next.

- I use drawing to make a record of my ideas and experiences.

- To help me think about my artwork, I collect and think about images (pictures), objects and other information linked to my ideas and what I want to do.

- I use a sketchbook to make a record of things I see, to plan my work and to experiment and improve my ideas.

- I make good choices of resources and references to help me develop my ideas.

- I use my sketchbook and drawing thoughtfully so that my work does improve my understanding and ideas and it helps me plan a piece of artwork. (For instance, my sketchbook shows several different versions of an idea and people can see how research has led to improvements in my artwork.)

- I can take part in research and exploration as I think of and develop my own personal ideas

- I confidently use my sketchbook for different purposes including: recording my observations; developing ideas; testing materials; planning my artwork and recording information.

- I can work independently to develop a range of ideas which show curiosity, imagination and originality

(Jennings, 2006, reproduced with permission)

Assessing children beyond levels in Art and Design

The notion of assessment in Art and Design has developed over time in relation to published curriculum documents and political expectations (Hopper, 2007). Since the arrival of the current National Curriculum (DfE, 2013), there is no longer a standard measure being used in all schools. As the previous system of 'levelling' a pupil's progress has been replaced by a range of different approaches, some schools have defined their own approaches, others have purchased 'off the peg' solutions and regrettably others have ignored the need to assess across the curriculum and focused their energies on a restricted number of subjects (and possibly omitted Art and Design altogether).

Too often, assessment in the subject has been undertaken as a simplified checklist of what has been covered in the curriculum plan with little attention paid to the learning experiences that have been gained in the process. Little wonder then, that many teachers have failed to grasp the importance of good assessment practice. As a consequence, some recent commercial publishers of assessment software have produced and sold their materials ready populated with just the bullet points of the National Curriculum document. As we have already noted several times, this is not

Figure 7.2 Example assessment sheet from ENViL

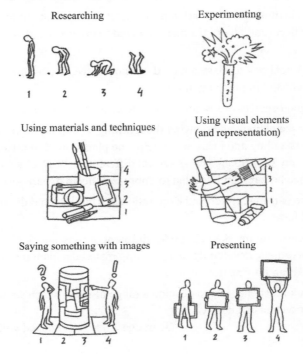

sufficiently robust to plan from or to assess with and teachers aiming for mastery will be uncomfortable settling for these overly simplified approaches.

Across mainland Europe, the European Network for Visual Literacy (ENViL) at the time of writing is still working on a similar assessment structure (Wagner and Schönau, 2016) to that defined by China and Gast (2014), but defining the areas as essentially two forms of visual reflection: art production (encompassing generating ideas and making) and art reception (including evaluating and knowledge). The intention is to produce a series of materials that could be adapted and used by teachers across Europe to best suit the demands of their country's curriculum. An example of an early draft is included here (see Figure 7.2). (An adaptable digital version can be obtained from http://envil.eu.)

What does assessment actually look like in primary Art and Design?

Let's consider several elements of assessment in turn – starting with teachers' understanding and the expectations they communicate to each other as well as their pupils. In 1997, the government published a booklet entitled *Expectations in Art at Key Stages 1 and 2*. It did not attempt to set out a staged set of expectations to use as a measurement tool, but it did set out to exemplify standards for pupils at the end of Key Stages 1 and 2 by providing annotated illustrations of pupils' work 'to support planning, teaching and assessment' (SCAA, 1997: 2). Sadly, the booklet is now out of print but the principles it suggested are still helpful today. In schools where good assessment takes place, there will be a clear understanding of the intended achievements when planning for the long term (defining what will be expected across the whole school), the medium term (in given year groups across the academic year) and the short term (in the lesson plans). In order to support the planning process, a school portfolio of pupils' work is particularly helpful as it also helps the less-experienced teachers to understand what the quality of work produced by children might look like. This same process remains in the best schools today; there will be a school portfolio that illustrates the kind of work pupils have produced, with a wide range of materials and media across each year group and therefore across the whole school. These may be linked to the particular projects and themes that have been defined in the long-term curriculum map (see also Chapter 8) and can be used to generate discussion, comparison and challenge expectations across the staff team. Some examples of pupils' artworks can be found throughout this book, indicating the kinds of collections that could be built into a portfolio. We want to emphasize that both 2D and 3D experiences can (and ought to) be assessed and that there are some emerging indications that children's skills in both areas develop at very different rates (Pataky, 2018) – to each other and importantly perhaps, also from those recorded in the past. If we are to assess well, we will need to update our understanding. (See Figures 7.3 and 7.4.)

Where a portfolio is constructed in discussion between pupils and their teacher, a rich source of assessment information is shared together. In her work on portfolios, Pereira de Eça (2005: 211) identified a series of possible forms of data that could be discussed and collected in this way:

- reports or notes (visual or written) of previous experiences, interests, etc.;
- final visual products – images of paintings, photographs, films, videos, installations, exhibitions, etc.;

Figures 7.3 and 7.4 Understanding KS1 pupils' processes and expectations

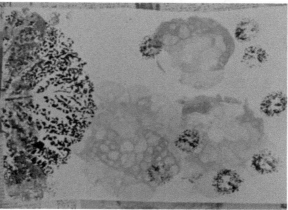

- visual or written preliminary studies, developmental records;
- investigation reports, data, critical inquiry (written and visual); and
- self-assessment reports – including interviews, tapes, video, digital records of the students' intentions, progress, investigations, achievements, presentations, etc.

Next, how important is it to retain some contextual understanding of the lesson(s) in which the finished artwork was produced? Let's take a specific example of some pencil drawings produced by a class of Year 6 pupils in one well-meaning primary school. Each year, the class was asked to draw a shoe and the teacher and art subject leader used the collection to judge the progress made across the class. Examples of such drawings are reproduced here (see Figures 7.5–7.8).

How helpful could this evidence be for the staff? There might be some merit in analysing the drawings for indications of the use of tonal representation, confidence in recording lines, originality of viewpoint presented, accuracy of the representation recorded or scale of the drawing. All of these could be viewed as valid aspects to consider, but if they did not directly relate to the focus of the lesson or objective articulated by the teacher, then such 'assessment' becomes a very questionable activity. The drawings reproduced here illustrate this as we do not know what was given as instruction or the expectation communicated by the teacher so we can only speculate. (In fact, as the task was finally introduced by a supply teacher, we may not know the context of form of instruction that day.) Would these drawings help us to gain a fuller idea of the pupil's interests and artistic abilities? In all honesty, probably not. The best we might be able to deduce is the way in which each drawing

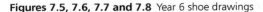

Figures 7.5, 7.6, 7.7 and 7.8 Year 6 shoe drawings

was attempted and built by looking carefully at the guidelines used or erased from the final image. To understand more would require the harvesting of information from the adult(s) who were present as it was made. How confident did the pupil appear? Where did they make their first mark on the paper? How challenging did they find the task? And how long did they take to complete it? The importance of first-hand observation in Art and Design lessons really cannot be overemphasized as it allows a far more accurate and deeper understanding of the four progress objectives (referred to above) than can otherwise be constructed. Good primary teachers of Art and Design, watch very carefully at the time of the activity and learn to target their questions towards this end: poor teachers rely only on the artworks collected in at the end of the lesson.

Another example of misunderstanding by the adult affecting the pupil's learning experience can be observed in Figure 7.9. On the face of it, a young pupil playfully explores one of the sixteen cast-iron figures produced by the sculptor Peter Burke (*Assembly*, 2001). The photograph was taken moments before the supervising adult reprimanded him for not adhering to the teacher's expectations. All of the sensory experiences – including feeling the rough texture of the metal and smelling the odour of the iron oxide, besides the development of understanding the construction process

Figure 7.9 A rich learning experience?

that he might have gleaned were in effect brushed aside. The reason for this is in the bottom right hand corner of the photograph where clipboard and paper can be seen. The teacher had wanted the class to observe and draw. The supervising adult was unable to link the benefit of the activities to the deeper learning being enacted before their eyes but instead focused on a particular outcome that might have been used for a remote assessment activity later. Unfortunately, this is not an uncommon mistake.

Green and Mitchell (1997) constructed a diagrammatic model to illustrate the relationship between effective assessment and the process of children's art-making – what they described as 'the reflective spiral'. We have revised this in Figure 7.10.

The kinds of 'key questions' suggested are designed both to elicit a deeper understanding and to provide a frame for further development. For example, Type A questions might include 'How is your idea coming along?', which encourages talk about the development of the design. These can be widened to allow other pupils to participate and share their ideas as well and provides insights into the processes of looking, thinking and doing. Or 'Do you want (or need) to practise more (or find out more about this material)?'. These are helpful for those who seem to be struggling with particular media in order to encourage them to experiment more and build their confidence. This stage is often omitted by teachers whose confidence level is low and they feel the need to rush towards a predetermined outcome – but this may be at the cost of never adequately building understanding or confidence, which will have repercussions at other times. Or, 'What do you think is going to happen next?' This kind of question draws out the existing level of the child's understanding and encourages an organization and formulation of new possibilities. Type B questions should aim to allow connections to be made by pupils between their own work and that of others – especially the work of artists. They could include, 'Have you thought about artists who work in this way?' The role of the teacher as a knowledgeable other aiding the development of the pupil's understanding becomes clear at this point. Teachers might need to have a ready-prepared list of resource materials to hand to prompt and discuss further. The Type C questions move the discussion towards a summative conclusion. They might include, 'Do you think the work is finished now? Or is there more that you think you could do? What do you really like about your piece? Can

Figure 7.10 The reflective assessment spiral

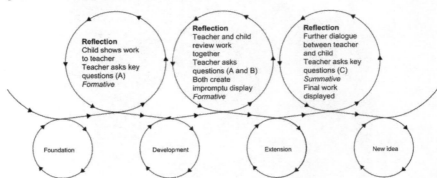

you tell me what you have learned about the language of art (e.g. colour, line, form, pattern, texture, etc.) in doing this? Have you achieved what you hoped to achieve? What else might you do to develop this in a different way?'

All of these questions benefit the understanding of both teacher and child. They should not be used as a checklist to demonstrate the activity has been completed, but as the enriching opportunity described by Alexander (2006) as 'dialogic teaching'. At all stages of this 'reflective spiral', the pupil's confidence is being built, allowing a gradual transfer to even higher levels in the next project they undertake, and even when moving beyond the primary school into secondary provision (and perhaps even beyond this too). There are many other models of the types of questions that could be used and developed in the KS2 classroom – including those suggested by Jennings (2006). These are grouped under the headings of the previous National Curriculum (QCA, 1999) but are still helpful for teachers who are unsure how to frame questions for children. (Only a sample is included here – the full document can be downloaded from the website given at the end of this chapter.)

Exploring and developing ideas: pupils should be able to answer these questions well:

- What information from your research did you choose to help you to develop your work?
- Why did you select this information?

Investigating and making art, craft and design: pupils should be able to answer these questions well:

- What features of 'X' (the 'thing' your artwork is about) affected your choice of materials and art techniques?
- What materials and art techniques did you use? How did you combine materials and techniques? Explain how you combined and organized shape, form and space, and applied colour, tone, pattern and texture in your artwork.

Evaluating and developing work: pupils should be able to answer these questions well:

- Describe and explain the ideas, methods and techniques you used to create your own artwork.
- What different ideas, methods and techniques did others use?
- How did the artists' choices relate to the purpose and context of the artwork?
- How did you adapt and refine your work to reflect your view of its purpose and meaning?

(Jennings, 2006, reproduced with permission)

Planning for progression

As we've noted, assessment and planning are closely linked, and they can be utilized further by aiding and demonstrating the progression made by pupils. Our experience suggests that, without a robust understanding of the subject, the important aspect of progression can be lost. China (n.d.: 8) suggests a number of issues through which progression might be understood and observed:

- gain in pupils' confidence;
- extension of their repertoire of technical skills and techniques;
- developed and extended research skills;
- pursuing ideas of increasing intellectual challenge, complexity and depth;
- their response to (and use with increasing sensitivity) the formal visual elements of art such as shape, tone, colour, line, texture, etc.;
- increased knowledge of art and artists;
- use of materials with increasing imagination and sensitivity;
- taking of risks, and embracing creative and imaginative responses; and
- working with increasing independence.

China also makes some very pertinent comments about progression. Firstly, that progression in the subject 'lies in the application rather than the acquisition of skills'. This is an increasingly common issue in primary schools where the weakened knowledge and understanding of the subject has resulted in simplistic checklists of skills that teachers will use to assess pupils. Without a robust underpinning of such knowledge, it is easy to focus instead on the nature of materials or techniques pupils use rather than the increased complexity of the tasks and challenges expected of them. Therefore when progress is defined as a list of specific materials and processes to be worked through in a particular order, or as a sequence of techniques in the use of the formal visual elements (line, tone, colour, etc.), then it can be deduced that the teachers' subject knowledge needs to be improved.

The three important aspects of progress that teachers can plan effectively are by:

- **increasing the breadth of content** by providing rich opportunities for pupils to respond, participate and engage;
- **increasing pupils' depth of knowledge and understanding** of the language of the subject, materials and processes as well as the way in which art has been viewed across the world over time;
- **improving the quality of pupils' responses** and the outcomes through the development of practical and technical skills as well as their ability to reflect on, adapt and improve their work and critically evaluate the work of artists, craftspeople and designers.

These aspects will be frequently found in the pages of this book as they drive our passion for ensuring the mastery of Art and Design in primary schools.

Quick pause moment – *Thinking about progression*:

- How would you define progression in Art and Design?
- How might you evidence that (especially to colleagues, parents or inspectors)?
- How would your pupils define progress? How much correlation would there be with your own definition? (Can you explain this?)

What about the inspectors' view?

We have deliberately left this until now as we felt it was important to set the scene carefully and not cause a panic about assessment behaviours without first making links to the aspects of good practice referred to above. The Office for Standards in Education, Children's Services and Skills (Ofsted) has reported on assessment in Art and Design in a number of reports, particularly the subject survey inspections (Ofsted 2009, 2012), an evaluation of good practice in the subject (Ofsted, 2003) and an evaluation of Assessment for Learning (AfL) in the curriculum (Ofsted, 2008).

Summarizing comments from all these reports, Ofsted inspectors have noted:

- Effective assessment in the subject is often hampered by teachers themselves.
- Teachers' weak subject knowledge, appreciation of standards expected and understanding of progression all affect the application and use of good assessment.
- Insufficient differentiation in Art and Design restricts the level of challenge for pupils and constrains their progress and creativity.
- Too often the long-term impact on pupils' attainment and progress – both in Art and Design and across other areas of the curriculum was negligible.
- Rather than viewed as an opportunity for promoting creative skills, assessment was sometimes viewed as a hindrance to creativity.

It is also worth considering the expectations provided in the overview prepared for non-specialist inspectors (Ofsted, 2014):

Expectations of **pupils** in art, craft and design relate to:

- perception and observation;
- manipulation and practice;
- communication and drawing;
- knowledge and understanding;
- attitudes and approaches; and
- appreciation and application.

By the end of the **Early Years Foundation Stage** children should be able to:

- show curiosity in visual and tactile stimuli and in their own discoveries;
- explore digital, 2D, 3D media, large and small scale, inside and outside;
- express imagination and record observations through drawing;
- develop interest in the work of people who create art, craft and design;
- concentrate when challenged by the unfamiliar; and
- cooperate well with adults and other children when working collaboratively.

By the end of **Key Stage 1** pupils should be able to:

- collect visual and tactile stimuli discriminately, for creative purposes;
- use a wide range of media expressively and show developing control of tools and techniques;
- use sketchbooks effectively to capture observations, ideas, experiences including drawing;
- distinguish between artists, craft-makers and designers;
- sustain interest and inquiry to develop skills and widen knowledge; and
- understand how art, craft and design makes an impact on everyday life.

By the end of **Key Stage 2** pupils should be able to:

- recognize qualities of line, colour, shape, pattern, texture and form in different stimuli;
- improvise effectively with limited materials and show increasing confidence with specific media;
- use sketchbooks regularly to revisit, review and refine their work, including drawing;
- make connections between their own work and knowledge of other creative practitioners;
- respond skilfully, creatively and with resilience to challenges set by teachers or other adults; and
- understand how art, craft and design is applied in unfamiliar contexts and cultures.

Effective provision for art, craft and design in primary schools:

- is supported by clear planning for pupils' progression of skills, knowledge and understanding;
- teaches pupils how to revisit, review and refine prior learning in addition to 'new' experiences;
- approaches drawing from a range of starting points, media and for different purposes;

Figures 7.11 and **7.12** Felt-making or drawing with wire

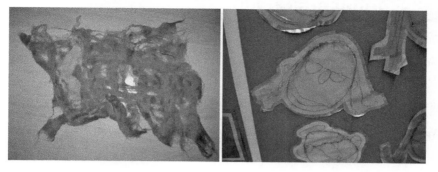

- familiarizes pupils with visual concepts through their work and that of creative practitioners;

- uses 'live' projects to teach pupils how art, craft and design is applied in different contexts; and

- integrates visits to art galleries or work with visiting practitioners skilfully into pupils' learning. (See Figures 7.11 and 7.12.)

Throughout this chapter, we have tried to maintain our focus on the development of mastery in primary Art and Design. The issues noted by inspectors (which have been summarized here) have been reflected a number of times throughout the whole book. We have presented the best practice in each chapter in order to inspire readers and invite application in the classroom. In every instance, we would argue there are strong links between teaching, assessment and learning, developing from and continually feeding into the assessment processes we have described above. Teachers who master these links may well be amazed at the artworks their pupils create.

Further help and support

Over recent years, assessment has increasingly become associated with reporting pupils' progress in the core subjects. Further changes and developments are to be expected over the next few years (and possibly until the next curriculum review). There are a number of helpful sources of information that have maintained a view of the importance of gathering the best insights in assessment in Art and Design. In addition to those listed at the end of the book, we would like to highlight these website sources and the materials available from them:

National Society for Education in Art and Design (NSEAD) www.nsead.org
Expert Subject Advisory Group for Art and Design (ESAG) https://esag4art.com
Dan China (formerly Senior Inspector in Buckinghamshire) http://danchina.net
Mr Jennings (Assistant Headteacher, Westdale Junior School) www.MrJennings.co.uk

Recommended reading

The following three texts are suggested as follow-on reading:

China, D. and Gast, G. (2014), *The National Curriculum for Art and Design Guidance: EYFS, Primary KS1–2*. Corsham: NSEAD. Available from www.nsead.org [accessed November 2017].

Hopper, G. (2007), 'Assessment of Art and Design in the Primary School' T. Rayment, (ed.), *The Problem of Assessment in Art and Design*. Bristol: Intellect. pp. 27–39.

Wagner, E. and Schönau, D. (eds) (2016), *Common European Framework of Reference for Visual Literacy*. Münster: Waxmann.

Chapter 8
Practical Issues

This chapter considers the practical issues surrounding the teaching and learning of Art and Design, from the consideration of how teachers engage in planning the curriculum through to the issues of resources and of health and safety concerning such practical activities.

The following are discussed:

- Important considerations when planning Art and Design.
- Why progression is important.
- How best to tackle the lack of resources; and what resources are required.
- Health and safety considerations for practical activities.
- Consideration of the classroom environment (when teaching Art and Design).
- How to utilize other adults in the Art and Design process.

Important considerations when planning Art and Design

In the current education regime schools are expected to design and publish their curriculum on their website. Since the introduction of the revised National Curriculum (Department for Education (DfE), 2013) a number of schools have taken the opportunity to consider and redevelop their curriculum offer – considering pedagogical questions about the way subjects are taught, as well as the skills and knowledge intended coverage across the curriculum. There have also been a number of publishers who have created completely new schemes claiming to cover the entire National Curriculum (DfE, 2013), such as *Inspire Curriculum* (Cornwall Learning, 2016) or *Dimensions Curriculum* (Creative Curriculum Design, 2016), for schools to purchase and use. We do not want to suggest that purchasing a preplanned curriculum is actually required or that one model is better than the other, but there are some important factors to consider. These may be helpful for gauging the appropriateness of a published curriculum, as well as evaluating a school's own designed one. When engaging in the Art and Design elements of the curriculum we must consider the skills, understanding, knowledge and opportunities to be offered in order to ensure an enthralling and engaging curriculum that inspires and challenges pupils with clear progression throughout (DfE, 2013). In this book we have tried to demonstrate both why and how this might be achieved in schools. The curriculum should also be relevant, adaptive and meet the needs of the current pupil population, as well as embracing new opportunities in local provision or national projects (e.g. a temporary art exhibition or national celebratory event). Children should have an opportunity to develop skills in both two- and three-dimensional work, including drawing, painting, sculpture, textiles, printing, mixed media and also, importantly, digital and developing technologies. Planning should consider the opportunities for children to learn from and about artists, designers, craft-makers and architects from their own culture and the cultures of others (DfE, 2013). If this is to be achieved, careful preparation is needed, building experiences across the school's planning processes – in long- and medium-term plans. Enabling children to progress each year, consolidating, developing and exploring new knowledge within these areas.

> ## Quick pause moment – *Thinking about art education experiences*:
>
> Consider your experiences of teaching art:
>
> - What media or artists are you most familiar with?
> - Do children have opportunities to work with a wide range of media?

Why progression is important

When considering the content of the Art and Design curriculum it is important the school considers the range of experiences for each child throughout their learning journey, with particular attention to the progression of skills. Progression should be considered within each stage of planning from the long term to the individual lesson components. This progression is sometimes lacking within the Art and Design curriculum, where schools and teachers have come under increased pressure to perform within core subjects, leaving the art lesson to become a one-off activity seen as a treat or as a way to beautify the school environment (Ogier, 2017). Although progression is crucial, if children are to have high quality art experiences that enable them to develop their ability to express themselves, their skills and their knowledge of the subject, they need teachers who understand the mastery processes. The notions of self-expression, imagination and exploration, and their important relationship to Art and Design have already been discussed in Chapter 5, but, unless teachers plan for opportunities to explore these areas, children will not necessarily progress across their primary career.

Long-term planning

Long-term planning in the Art and Design curriculum should identify 'what a student is to know and/or be able to do with respect to some body of content at the end of some designated instructional period' (Eisner, 2002: 159). This form of planning is the journey that the child will take throughout their time across the primary years, from which the school will identify key objectives for the child to achieve. Long-term planning ought to reflect the National Curriculum (DfE, 2013; National Society for Education in Art and Design (NSEAD), 2014a), but also may display greater depth of the areas and concepts to be explored. (Medium-term planning is based on these long-term objectives. Teachers should consider these objectives and relate them to the theme or topic to enable their achievement.) Long-term planning ought to identify and reflect the ethos of the subject as well as the consideration of the content to be taught – including such details as artists or movements, cultures or even particular materials to work with. This should ensure children have a broad and balanced curriculum experience within Art and Design, accessing a range of materials, process and artists, throughout their primary education.

In this process of planning, teachers often identify outcomes that are clearly linked with measurable objectives, but with Art and Design teachers should additionally consider a key feature, which is the 'encouragement of improvisation and the cultivation of a personal rendering of one's ideas' (Eisner, 2002: 160). This cultivation of ideas can enable a rich, reflexive and responsive curriculum, with clearly defined objectives, which enables the pupils to develop their personal expression and thought processes in relation to their own work. This 'encouragement of improvisation' does not mean a lack of planning, instead it is planning that allows for the personal, the individualized exploration of ideas, without teachers visualizing specific outcomes (Edwards, 2013). In this way, a truly creative curriculum can be both planned and experienced.

Medium-term planning

Medium-term plans are the more detailed plans, either defining the unit of work being taught within a term or a particular time period such as an arts week. These plans are more detailed throughout, identifying objectives for each lesson with clear outcomes that are linked to aspects of planned assessment. Although the format for such plans varies from school to school, Figure 8.2 is an example from a school that decided to redesign the whole curriculum (and is discussed in more detail in the case study below, p. 140).

The National Curriculum (DfE, 2013) clearly states that Art and Design should involve children in 'exploring their ideas' (2013: 177) so medium-term plans should

Figure 8.1 Art exhibition in a school hall

include objectives that enable the children to explore and express their ideas. These could be termed as 'expressive outcomes', which 'are the outcomes that students realise in the course of a curriculum activity' (Eisner, 2002: 161). These expressive outcomes ensure pupils' work reflects the self, so the nature of the art outcomes across a whole class can be particularly individualized and delightfully varied. Problem-solving objectives can offer children the opportunity to work within a specific area, but also the freedom to explore and resolve the challenges using their own ideas and creative nature, highlighting the very nature of design (Eisner, 2002). (See Figure 8.1.)

Quick pause moment – Case study: School planning

School Medium term planning

A medium-size school in a rural area with a mixed demographic of children and a range of needs is currently performing above national averages across the board. They decided to redesign their curriculum as a whole to enable greater opportunities for cross-curricular learning, to capture and hook the children's fascination and passion for learning across the subjects, alongside the ability to offer a supportive curriculum to suit the needs of their demographic group. A number of the children are lacking in rich cultural life experiences, which impacts on both language development and aspirations. The curriculum process involved developing an overarching area of study for each term, identified in the long-term plan. (See Figure 8.2.)

Figure 8.2 An example long-term plan

	Term 1 Home and Away	New Beginnings/Democracy	Term 2 Block History	Remembrance Day	Term 3 Environment Explorers	Anti bullying	Term 4 Going Global	Enterprise and Charity	Term 5 Time Tunnel	Healthy Living/Sports Week	Term 6 Making the News	Transition. Moving on, Meta cognition, Aspirations
Year F	Our school, Local area		Being different, My life, My family		Explorers		Grow your own		Dinosaurs, Space travel		Emergency services	
Year 1	Harty		Freedom Summer		Aquatics		Eco warriors/ Going green		School days/Vile Victorians		Fire	
Year 2	Eastchurch		Mary Seacole		Deserts		Totally tourist		WW1/ WW2		Flooding	
Year 3	Shearness		Rosa Parks		Mountains		Feeding people around the world		Eccentric Egyptians		Volcanos/ Earthquakes	
Year 4	Minster		Martin Luther King		Polar Regions		Climate commotion		Terrible Tudors		Storms and hurricanes	
Year 5	Queenborough		Nelson Mandela		Rainforest		Human rights/ wrongs		Awesome Aztecs		Drought and famine	
Year 6	Bluetown		Barack Obama		Rainforest		Global branding		Vicious Vikings		Refugees/ Migrants Disasters in our own country	

The long-term plan spans the academic year, and a child's journey through school, from which the medium-term plans were created with key areas of learning selected. This long-term plan enables opportunities for whole-school activities and relevant links to enable sharing of learning across the year groups. This can be seen from the overarching themes that span all years. These areas of learning included such things as 'our locality, sustainability and environmental' from which year groups developed a theme to which most subjects related.

Some of the challenges of designing such a curriculum are selecting the appropriate subject knowledge to be taught within each theme alongside ensuring progression and coverage of knowledge and skills. When designing the Art and Design medium-term plans to sit within the curriculum overview the school were mindful of two aspects.

These were firstly the need to ensure that process and progression was built across the lessons and secondly to incorporate a wide range of artists and designers from different cultures working in a range of media. They particularly wished to move away from the school's previous practice of focusing on a diet of historical male European artists (Cox and Watts, 2007), a common experience in primary schools that can often be linked to the level of the teacher's subject knowledge and confidence.

The medium-term planning format (Figure 8.3 and back of the book) highlights a number of key areas. These include links to the National Curriculum (2013), identification of artists with a range of suggested artworks (ensuring teachers focus on a range of work not a single picture), resources required, opportunities for visits, media and processes, as well as key skills knowledge and language to be taught. The skeleton of the medium-term plan for each theme, which identifies these processes, artists and subject knowledge, was developed by the Art and

Design subject leader, a specialist in the field. Teachers then had the opportunity to develop and personalize the learning to reflect the needs of their class. This was to support the teachers' subject knowledge introducing them to new artists and processes.

Figure 8.3 School medium-term planning

Year 6					
Yearly overview for Art and Design Technology					
Term 1	Term 2	Term 3	Term 4	Term 5	Term 6
Bluetown	Barack Obama	Rainforest	Global Branding	Vicious Vikings	Refugees/Migrants /Disasters
Art: Pen and ink - abstraction	Art: Artist portfolios	Art: Printing	D&T: Product Design	Art: Textiles	D&T: Food
National Curriculum:					

Art: Key stage 2
Pupils should be taught to develop their techniques, including their control and their use of materials, with creativity, experimentation and an increasing awareness of different kinds of art, craft and design.
Pupils should be taught:
▯ to create sketch books to record their observations and use them to review and revisit ideas
▯ to improve their mastery of art and design techniques, including drawing, painting and sculpture with a range of materials [for example, pencil, charcoal, paint, clay]
▯ about great artists, architects and designers in history.

This medium-term planning format is just one example: there are many different ones. Schools have the opportunity to personalize them to suit their requirements and each format has particular strengths. This example format ensures teachers understand the delivery of a process. It also ensures a broad range of artists is included within each medium-term plan, even identifying suitable images to share, and this supports the non-specialist Art and Design teacher. Bowden et al. (2013) suggest it is important to support the teaching team, motivating and inspiring them to deliver high-quality lessons. Medium-term plans can be detailed in such a way that teachers may find there is less requirement for individual lesson plans.

With the subject coordinator overseeing plans in this detail, whole-school progression can be clearly seen as well as the opportunities for monitoring the practice across the different year groups. Ofsted, 2008) identified that where Art and Design provision was of high quality it stemmed from effective subject leaders with strong knowledge and a passion for their subject area. This was clearly evident within this school, with the added bonus of an ethos of valuing the arts across the whole curriculum. By suggesting artists and using a range of artworks, teachers were encouraged to embrace the fullest impact on both their and the children's knowledge of artists.

As a teacher what can I do about the lack of resources?

Resources are always a challenge in the primary classroom when engaging with practical activities. The current funding climate in schools has done little to reduce these challenges. Teachers need to be creative, considering options that are cost-effective yet still enable the fullest access to explore the curriculum. There are many art projects children can engage in using a range of recycled resources, such as plastic bottles, cardboard boxes and naturally occurring, found objects. These projects can be stimulated or supported by the many artists who create their work using recycled or found objects. Land artists Andy Goldsworthy or Richard Long are both contemporary artists working with naturally occurring, found materials, often those available in the landscape itself. Land Art was a movement that emerged mainly in the UK and the USA around the 1960s, using, as the name suggests, materials from the land. Richard Long's installation of found leaves, *A Circle in the Amazon* (2016), demonstrates how the found objects can form a sculpture, which considers colour, form and pattern. Children could use Richard Long or Andy Goldsworthy to inspire their own Land Art installations, using found objects within the school grounds. Or they could investigate and sculpt using everyday materials. Figure 8.4 shows children's work produced from observing cultural art form by artists creating large wooden Tiki. The children then created their own interpretations using only pencil and paper, but very effectively moved into 3D to form these sculptures (i.e. the children's sculptures). The sculpture utilizes the properties of the materials with colour and form both playing a vital role.

Recyclable materials are a fantastic opportunity for creating artwork. Teachers could draw inspiration from artists such as El Anatsui, a Ghanaian sculptor recognized internationally for his large-scale installations using materials such as tin

Figure 8.4 Paper sculptures

Figures 8.5 and 8.6 Sculpture from recycled objects

cans and bottle tops, or Czech artist Veronica Richterova, who creates sculptures by manipulating plastic bottles into a range of forms by cutting, heating or twisting. Richterova's *Mushrooms* (2005) or *Penguins* (2008) show how a simple throw away resource can form an inspiring sculpture, enabling children to work at a range of scales for very limited costs. Both artists are internationally recognized, creating a wealth of work from the everyday objects that might otherwise be thrown away. With the work of El Anatsui there is also an element of cultural identity explored, with references to his own cultural heritage. He says, 'art grows out of each particular situation, and I believe that artists are better off working with whatever their environment throws up'. This highlights that, for creative teachers or artists, there is an ability to make art with whatever is to hand, be it recycled card, paper, plastics or items children have collected, including from the natural world.

Figures 8.5 and 8.6 show how children have taken inspiration from everyday objects, in this case using plastic bottles to create individual flowers, which have then been joined together to form the larger installation. Children firstly explored and developed their skills in making the individual flowers, learning how to mould and shape the plastic, before using these skills to create personalized individual flowers, all of which were different. Finally, the children combined them to create a tree installation of flowers, a striking sculpture enhanced through bringing the individual elements to form a group. The nature of the resources led children to experiment and the low cost enabled the children and teachers to take risks, confident that if the flowers failed, then the resource costs would be minimal.

What resources are useful within the primary school?

An Art and Design resource list in a primary school could potentially be endless so the suggestions below are simply to provoke some consideration of the possibilities of what would be useful for developing a broad and balanced curriculum. Often there will be other resources lurking in school cupboards and, at times, teachers will have to be creative and use whatever they find there. When purchasing resources, the best approach is to consider the long-term plans and ensure the materials being ordered will resource these activities.

Drawing materials

There are many options when we consider materials for drawing and it is important to ensure children are exposed to a wide range of these materials in their Art and Design experience. Bowden et al. (2013) warn of the difficulties of introducing too many drawing materials at once, which can impact and limit the child's ability to become proficient in the media they are using. This means teachers must invest time to enable children to master the skills and potential of each medium before introducing the complexities of another medium. There is a wide range of inexpensive drawing media such as charcoal (charcoal can be freely made in a fire which could form part of the forest school curriculum), graphite sticks, inks, felt-tip pens of all thicknesses, chalks, oil pastels, digital tools (including 3D styluses), handwriting pens and of course the pencil, ranging from the very hard 9H through the standard writing HB through to a very soft 9B. Varieties of coloured pencils are available – some are more sophisticated and can create washes by also using water, others are chunky to enable good grip for small hands or for those with poor fine motor skills. These resources may only be required as a school set, while other children might want to access some of them on a daily basis, depending on pupils' age, curriculum and, of course, level of teacher understanding.

Painting materials

The most common paints found in the primary classroom are bottled ready-mixed poster paints in a variety of colours. These are inexpensive and can be used in a variety of ways – for example, consider adding PVA glue to increase the viscosity and coverage quality if using on models or plastics. Consider how children will want (or be allowed) to use paints: we have already noted the benefits of restricting colour palettes. There are many other paints to choose from, including tins of watercolours, acrylic, fabric paint, powder paint or compressed powder blocks. Most forms can be found in schools. Acrylic is the least common, but it is particularly useful for three-dimensional work, for example painting ceramics or models, as it has effective coverage and can be opaque. While slightly more expensive it is really worth the investment. Consider also other resources to support painting processes: brushes of mixed sizes and handle length (long brushes are more challenging to control, so do remember this when selecting brushes for young children), various papers or card, palette knives, water pots and mixing palettes. The last two can often be substituted with recycling materials such as yogurt pots (although they will not be as sturdy or durable). Cardboard palettes can be a single-use solution. Used newspaper has traditionally been used to cover the surface of the tables, but many schools have invested in plastic table clothes as an alternative protective covering. All of these can affect or reduce the amount of clearing-up time required at the end of a lesson.

Sculptural materials

The list of materials for making sculpture could potentially be endless. Many materials can be found for free, such as cardboard boxes, packaging, tubes, plastic bottles, fabrics and many other items. In our discussion of sculptural materials here we especially want to include clay, which is an inexpensive material available from educational suppliers (or in the school grounds if a friendly potter can help you find and prepare it!). Clay comes in different types and colours (depending on the minerals in it: red or iron oxide being the most common colourant in commercially prepared clay for school use). For most projects an inexpensive (red) terracotta or buff (grey) clay is all you require. This will dry very hard or can be fired if you have access to a kiln. The minerals may stain children's skin temporarily, and they can also stain table tops, so we would always recommend a table covering of some sort – a board or J-cloth for each child might be a good idea. We would strongly suggest avoiding air-hardening clay (which has a number of brand names) as this is difficult to work with, dries very quickly while working and often forms a dusty crumbling mess shortly after creation. You will always be able to tell the difference between air-drying clay and natural clay as the former has very small nylon fibres added to the clay in an attempt to strengthen it in the drying process. We have not found this to work, and the children's disappointment as their work breaks up is something that is better avoided. Remember that although terracotta or buff clay can go into a kiln to be fired, it does not have to. Bowden et al. (2013) highlight that there are times you would deliberately choose not to kiln-dry clay, for example when adding found objects or producing large-scale pieces. Figure 8.7 below shows the result of teachers exploring the use of clay for building blocks to develop a large-scale sculpture, following which the clay was re-bagged to use again. (Air-drying clay cannot be reused and is actually a much more expensive option!)

Other resources you need for clay can be inexpensive, such as clay tools or instead use plastic or old cutlery, lolly sticks, sponges, cloth to roll onto such as inexpensive J-cloths or recycled material. Rolling pins and other kitchen utensils such as cheese graters, garlic presses or sieves can be used to give interesting effects when clay is forced through them. If you do want to fire work, ask among the parental community as some will own or have access to a kiln; and most secondary schools have kilns and will be happy to support primary schools in firing their work.

Figure 8.7 Teachers' clay sculpture

Other sculptural materials might include Modroc, wood, fabric, newspapers, plastics, card, recycled junk modelling, willow withies, beads, wire for models (be careful with what and where you purchase though as some wire designed for outdoor use is galvanized, which is also poisonous and so should not be used with children). A range of these materials can be collected from their families or from the local community's recycling, such as cardboard from local shops etc. Useful tools for sculpture are wire cutters, cool melt glue guns, scissors (both for children and adults), staplers, boards and protective covers for children and tables.

Printing

With printing it is important to consider what is used to carry out the printing. It is possible to print from almost anything – from natural or found objects such as vegetables, seed pods, shells or toys, to mono prints, wood blocks, press print or surface rubbings – so long as there is good surface texture. Figure 8.8 shows an exploration with printing using plastic bags to print with, combined with Easy Print (compressed polystyrene), onto a range of different surfaces of varying colours, giving tone, texture and depth to the final piece. For printing water-based printing inks will be required (these come in a range of colours), rollers (both hard and sponge types), inking up trays ('plates'), polystyrene tiles for printing, paper, card and string for string block prints. Laminated plastic wallets can make effective mats for inking up on, as these are cost-effective and washable. Printing on inexpensive paper can enable children to refine and understand the process prior to printing on more expensive paper or other materials. You can also extend these printing processes to fabric

Figure 8.8 Exploration printing

inks, printing on cotton or silk, using an iron for fixing (ensure an electrical PAT test is completed if using an iron in school). Marbling is another form of printing for which you require marbling inks and water trays. Or a very simple form of printing for young children is bubble printing in a water tray: this is a watered-down paint mixture where children blow bubbles using straws and take simple prints, which can be very rewarding. If vegetable printing with young children, ensure they have a wide range to print, beyond the potato (which is durable but must be cut by an adult, which might not be desirable); using softer vegetables or fruit cut in half (such as carrot, okra, cabbage, celery, broccoli and cauliflower) makes for some interesting examples to investigate, as do apples or pears. Avoid very soft fruit!

Fabric

Various fabrics can be used in a range of ways, from a canvas to print or paint on, as medium for dyeing, or as a material to sew or stitch together to form objects, such as wall hangings or items to wear. If dyeing fabric, it is necessary to consider what the fabric is made from: cottons take dyes well, as will silk, but polyester is often far more difficult to dye. Fabrics are again something that can be recycled, so don't overlook the opportunity to request used fabrics to use in school, such as sheets, clothes, etc. from families. All can be reused in different forms, and purchasing cotton sheets can often be less expensive than buying fabric by the metre. If children are being taught to sew, consider the needles and cottons being used – are they fit for the intended purpose or the age of child? Are quality fabric scissors available in the classroom? Beads, sequins and feathers are all items that could be used to stitch onto fabric; and fabric glitter or paint are useful when decorating work.

If developing processes such as batik are being used, a cotton or silk fabric will be needed to work on, and a hot or cold wax method could be used depending on the age and ability of the children. Another method similar to that used for mud cloth could be used (a cloth that originates from Africa). This requires a very thick flour-and-water paste that is piped onto the cloth, using disposable piping bags for ease. The paste is left to dry, and then dye can be painted onto the cloth (but do not submerge it in dye). Leave it to dry again and then pick off the paste, leaving the original colour fabric underneath.

Digital

The digital device is now part of the everyday for children: for them the touch screen is the norm and many seem to learn to use the digital world before they can properly draw or write. The potential for digital technology must also be realized (and not avoided or ignored) within the Art and Design curriculum. Digital media as a valid art dimension ripe to explore is clearly evident in the contemporary art world with artists such as Duncan Campbell, Elizabeth Price or David Hockney all using digital technology to form their artworks. Introducing children to such artists who are using technology to stimulate and produce pieces is crucially important, so that they too consider the potential of technology for the creation of their own works. Using resources from contemporary galleries, such as the Saatchi or Tate Modern, can support this. Hewlett and March (2015) suggest that digital technologies can enable children to utilize innovative ways to develop their artistic processes, often enabling them to work at speed to create, capture and edit works of art, such as film, photography, drawing or animation. Bowden et al. suggest pupils can 'experiment freely by combining text, sound and images to express their ideas' (2013: 43). The digital resources children can actually use at school will be dictated by the technology available there. Consider the merit of using a variety of devices that can film, photograph, draw, paint and then edit (possibly on a different one). Enabling the children to gain confidence in a recording device in turn enables them to explore, take risks and innovate with the digital resources. Wood (2004) suggests that an iPad enables children to access a range of tools and apps that can aid the Art and Design process, enabling them further opportunities for creative development of their work. Although not all schools have iPads, there are other tablets that would afford the same opportunities – the benefits of either tablet or iPad enable the individual to access a range of digital resources quickly. An increasing range of apps are now available that can enhance work (such as 'ArtRage' or 'Sketch – Draw and Paint'), for drawing or painting or a digital mixture of both. (See Figures 8.9 and 8.10.) Children can use these to initiate

Figures 8.9 and **8.10** Artworks produced by nine-year-old pupils using ArtRage software

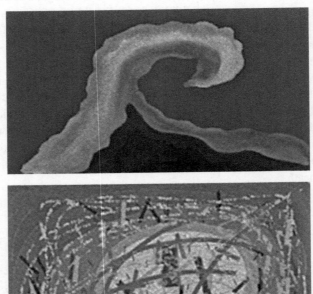

a piece of artwork or develop an existing work, thus embedding the technology into the process in different ways.

'Pic Collage' is a useful app for displaying images and creating inspiration boards or demonstrating a process, and there are also a number of film apps, such as iMovie, which can be used to develop short pieces of film that can be edited, adding in stills and sound etc. Whichever technologies are available within the school consider carefully the potential within the Art and Design processes. Hewlett and March (2015) observed that the use of technology motivated children to explore within their artwork, becoming playful with their use of technology to enhance the work. The more recent introduction of 3D printers will further enhance Art and Design: children will soon have the opportunity to draw and print their sculptures, design or models. On a smaller scale, 3D pens are reducing in costs and entering many primary classrooms – enabling children to make 3D drawings and giving instant form to their ideas.

Health and safety considerations

Teachers should always consider three aspects of health and safety within their Art and Design lessons:

- the space where the work is taking place;
- the resources, tools or materials being used;
- the children themselves.

Always be aware of the school's current Health and Safety policy. There may be particular aspects or materials within the curriculum that need careful consideration. (If in any doubt, we would recommend checking the Health and Safety information available on the NSEAD website where detailed expert advice is available.)

Space

To reduce risks when setting up the working space, consideration should be given to both how and where resources will be accessed. Consider the flow of children around the classroom and, if traffic jams or bottlenecks have been created to access the resources, be aware that these can lead to challenges that, at times, can result in children becoming less focused or fractious. Resources may be organized in trays that can be handed out or laid out at each workstation. This can also minimize unnecessary movement around the classroom, which in turn reduces these risks.

If a sink is required (and within the space) consider how many children it can facilitate at one time. What about the flooring that surrounds it – will it become a slip hazard when wet? If the teaching will be in a classroom with no sink, but water is required, consider setting up a wet area using buckets and trays to provide and capture the water.

Resources, materials and tools

Consider the resources and materials being used and ask what the potential risks are and how to minimize these. For certain materials or resources, it might be necessary to complete a school risk assessment form – this will be clear from the policy itself – but if in doubt or concerned it is always good to complete one. Materials such as types of glues, plaster of Paris products (including Modroc), dyes, clays and such materials as hot wax for batik might be in this group. If the material is considered to have too high a risk for the children concerned, consider if alternatives can be found or there might be ways to reduce the risk. For example, some primary teachers would consider lino printing a risky activity, often resulting in gouged fingers. Alternatives such as Easy Print (compressed polystyrene tiles) or string block prints give similar results but have lower risk factors. This notion of risk of resources will be dependent on the children being worked with – their ages, cognitive understanding and behaviour. (It should be said that lino printing could be carried out using a specialized bench hook and soft rubberized lino, with the processes being taught in small groups, which are more easily supervised.)

Tools

When using tools, observe and ensure all tools are in good working order. Is there any protective equipment that should be used with such tools? For example, when using a saw, are the saw blades secure and are the children using bench hooks? Can the children manage to use the bench hook, wood and saw together? When using scissors, are children handling and moving around the classroom safely with them? Are there tools that only adults working within the classroom should use? And, if so, how can we ensure only the adults have access to them? (As teachers, we have sometimes used a craft knife in our lessons – kept closed and safely stored in a pocket while not being used and then returned to be securely stored away at the end of the session.)

Children

It is very important to consider the actual children in the class(es) being worked with. Reflect on the task – is it suitable for their age or ability? Are there particular children within the class that need specific consideration due to their additional needs? (These could be linked to learning, physical or behavioural issues, so consider if any children with additional needs require the same or different resources to ensure their safety.)

For children with skin complaints you may need to offer the appropriate gloves, but check the best type for the child. (Latex ones would be additionally problematic if the child is allergic to latex!) Remember, if working outside the classroom at a distance from the first aid point, it would be wise to consider any particular medical needs the children have. For example, a child who has a severe allergic reaction might require immediate administration of medication, so check that the appropriate knowledge and medication are available where the activity is taking place. Children with asthma may need additional supervision when dust from Modroc or dry clay are airborne.

Consider when activities require protective clothing. This might just be to protect uniform from becoming dirty or damaged. Parents and children can both become upset and distressed if such care and attention has not been taken to protect their clothing in this way. Painting aprons or 'over cover shirts' should be accessible in school as most paints have the potential to stain if not treated correctly. Always use cold water to attempt to remove paint first, remembering that hot water is more likely to fix the colour!

Consideration of the classroom/school environment relating to Art and Design

Quick pause moment – *Thinking about Art and Design in the school environment*:

- When you last went into school what visual aspects to you remember?
- How might a school communicate their ethos around art?
- What do you feel the school environment tells you about the school?

The classroom/school environment can communicate the school's ethos and values to the whole community: it reflects the curriculum and the learning that the school values and engages with. With this in mind it is important to consider how the classroom environment could support teaching and learning in Art and Design. Does the school environment engage with and communicate the possibilities of Art and Design to the child? How is this done, and what Art and Design is evident around the school? These are important questions if we are to fully embrace and promote Art and Design across a school. If the school demonstrates value in the subject, children will feel more motivated and confident to work within it.

Cox and Watts (2007) suggest the classroom organization can ether open up possibilities for creative exploration and imagination within art or (more sadly) close them down. The surroundings and the availability of resources can both impact in this way. If children are to become creative and imaginative, then evidence of positive organization should be seen within the learning environment and resources, and the classroom layout should be used to support the creative process. Materials and resources need to be accessible to enable children to understand the media that are potentially available and to utilize them appropriately within their work. Consider the artistic processes already discussed and where and when children will need particular resources, such as paints, water, protective clothing and, importantly, safe storage or drying space.

Valuing the creative process both within the classroom and across the whole school is an invaluable way to ensure the children are motivated and have positive self-esteem in relation to art. Art and Design displays within the school should not only reflect the final outcomes of the artwork itself but also the creative process – which we believe to be just as important. The preliminary sketches or designs alongside versions of the final piece can all be displayed to enable different learners or observers to consider and understand the process engaged with, as well as demonstrating aspects of progress. Consider how to display 3D work in the school. (Figure 8.11 shows a school where sculpture is valued, with displays to enable them to share safely with the whole school.) A school art gallery space could potentially be incorporated into the environment, but it is important to consider how the work

Figure 8.11 How one school chose to display sculpture

shown represents both the children and the curriculum. And remember that, if work is not regularly reviewed and changed, it becomes 'wallpaper', with the children losing the ability to engage, and possibly becoming demotivated.

How can I utilize other adults in the Art and Design process?

Additional adults can take different roles in relation to Art and Design, whether a visiting expert artist practitioner, or a parent helper, or a regular classroom support professional (teaching assistant, TA). We need to consider how this additional adult can support the process. Additional adult support can be particularly useful with art and design for a range of reasons: there are often many resources to organize and/or move around the room, so extra hands can ensure this happens quickly and safely. Children can be supported with the range of resources and (possibly specialized) equipment to ensure they are using them appropriately. The additional adult may have a particular skill set or knowledge and expertise in Art and Design that can support and enhance the lesson. This might even involve them modelling the skill, particularly if their skills in a particular area are more developed than the teacher's. Using a knowledgeable 'other' in this way can benefit the skill acquisition and motivation of the children. Finally, the adult might have particular skills and knowledge enabling them to work very effectively with children with additional needs.

When working with additional adults within the classroom we need to ensure they have a clear understanding of the planned lesson objectives, the plan for learning, and any prerequisite knowledge, such as information about an artist or their works of art (which might also involve demonstrating key skills). Also we need to make sure they understand their role, which children they will support, what level of support might be expected, and just how much independence the child requires. As Cox and Watts point out 'the adult needs to be particularly sensitive to the kinds of intervention that are appropriate' (2007: 98), adults should therefore understand the personalized nature of Art and Design. Having the use of additional adults for Art and Design allows the teacher to take greater risks with media, scale and process. For example, working on 3D collaborative Modroc sculptures might be challenging with one teacher and thirty children but with the support of another it becomes a more achievable activity. This is similar with activities such as sewing, where a number of children may find fine motor skills and similar aspects challenging. The relationship is key when working alongside other adults, everyone needs to confident with their expectations and feel valued within the classroom. This involves the teacher either engaging the adult(s) in the planning process, which can be very effective, or ensuring there is time to share the expectations and outcomes of the lesson. Pre-teaching particular skills that the adult might require or ensuring there are opportunities initially to explore the media could be invaluable.

Conclusions

Throughout this chapter we have sought to inspire, reassure and challenge readers to engage with and explore a wider range of materials than they might otherwise feel confident with. Our reasoning for this has been that which has informed all the other chapters as well: we passionately believe that the children in our classrooms should have the very highest quality experiences in Art and Design. The best way to achieve this, we believe, is to invest in those who teach them. Our desire is that every reader has found something to further whet their appetite and that their curiosity will be reflected in their Art and Design lessons. Whether by thinking about particular artists, the materials that might be adapted and utilized, or the opportunities for children's collaborative learning, we hope that we have aided readers to master what we regard as the most exciting subject in the school curriculum!

Recommended reading

The following three texts are suggested as follow-on reading:

Bowden, J., Ogier, S. and Gregory, P. (2013), *The Art Subject Leader's Handbook*. London: Belair.

Cox, S. and Watts, R. (eds) (2007), *Teaching Art and Design 3–11*. London: Continuum.

Key, P. and Stillman, J. (2009), *Teaching Primary Art and Design*. Exeter: Learning Matters.

Afterword

Lesley Butterworth
General Secretary, National Society for Education in Art and Design

The National Society for Education in Art and Design (NSEAD) is the subject association, trade union and learned society for teachers and educators of art, craft and
design across all phases throughout the United Kingdom. As the voice of teachers
of our subject, we advocate for and celebrate art, craft and design, and welcome into
membership everyone who shares our values. Do look on our website for both further
information about our activities and a wealth of resources.

Vital to our work is developing a sustainable community of good practice, and key
to that is not only providing high-level continuing professional development opportunities and up-to-date resources but also ensuring the essential 'two-way traffic' of
forum and dialogue, talking with and listening to teachers and educators.

On behalf of NSEAD, I am delighted to recommend this book to everyone engaged
in teaching art, craft and design throughout the primary phase. It provides an essential and accessible text to support understanding of not only the material world of our
subject – tools, systems, techniques and skills – but also the pedagogy of our subject,
in order to nurture creativity and develop visual literacy, and an engagement in the
depth, breadth and value of art, craft and design. Essentially, it focuses upon not just
how but why we teach our subject.

For the Society, the importance of developing and supporting teachers at all stages
of their careers is at the core of our work. Teaching art, craft and design, like our
subject itself, is a work in progress and we seek to identify and ensure resources and
publications are up-to-date and of the highest standard.

What this engaging book does is give the teacher a holistic view of teaching our
subject, from health and safety to deploying staff, from materials and equipment to
realistically coping with a lack of the same. Assessment of our subject is carefully
considered – in a landscape without levels we consider why and how learning is
assessed, and what it tangibly looks like. Working with and arranging visits from
artists and organizing visits to museums and galleries are covered to ensure such
activities are both well organized and meaningful.

The book takes a position on creativity. Creativity is defined and located in
our subject but not solely by our subject. Within the context of teaching art, craft
and design we should never take creativity for granted as either a by-product or an

assumption. Teaching creatively and teaching to enable children to work creatively are two distinct activities and the authors take care to point this out.

Engagement in art, craft and design is fundamental to being human, to being visually and culturally aware and able to interact meaningfully in both material and virtual worlds.

It promotes personal fulfilment leading to a sense of belonging, a sense of worth, a sense of place and opportunities for careers, lifelong learning and leisure activities.

Art, craft and design is complex, and teaching and learning within and through our subject requires the authority and expertise that *Mastering Primary Teaching: Art and Design* carefully and joyfully delivers.

I warmly recommend it to everyone teaching our unique and incredible subject, and my sincere thanks to the authors for their commitment and energy in its creation.

NSEAD, 3 Masons Wharf, Potley Lane, Corsham, Wiltshire, SN13 9FY
Telephone: +44(0)1225 810134
E-mail: info@nsead.org
Website: http://nsead.org/

Alphabetical List of Artists Mentioned in the Text

Abts, Tomma	b. 1967	Hirst, Damien	b. 1965
Adams, Eddie	1993–2004	Höch, Hannah	1889–1978
Banksy	b. 1974	Hockney, David	b. 1937
Baselitz, Georg	b. 1938	Holt, Nancy	1930–2014
Braque, Georges	1882–1963	Hopper, Edward	1882–1967
Buess, Valérie	b. 1966	Kahlo, Frida	1907–1954
Burke, Peter	b. 1944	Kinder, Birgit	b 1949
Buttress, Wolfgang	b. 1965	Klee, Paul	1879–1940
Carle, Eric	b. 1929	Long, Richard	b. 1945
Cézanne, Paul	1839–1906	Marc, Franz	1880–1916
Dali, Salvador	1904–1989	Mehretu, Julie	b. 1970
da Vinci, Leonardo	1503–1506	Miro, Joan	1893–1983
de Goya, Francisco	1746–1828	Monet, Oscar-Claude	1840–1926
Delauney, Sonia	1885–1979	Moore, Henry	1898–1986
Duncan Campbell	1972	Morisot, Berthe	1841–1895
El Anatsui	1944	Morland, Natasha	b. 1973
Elizabeth Price	1966	O'Keefe, Georgia	1887–1986
el-Salahi, Ibrahim	b. 1930	Parker, Cornelia	b. 1956
Eriksen, Erik	1876–1959	Perry, Grayson	b. 1960
Escher, M.C.	1898–1972	Picasso, Pablo	1881–1973
Ford, Laura	b. 1961	Rae, Fiona	b. 1963
Forteza, Rafa	b. 1955	Riley, Bridget	b. 1931
Frankenthaler, Helen	1928–2011	Rothko, Mark	1903–1970
Gainsborough, Thomas	1727–1788	Rowe, Matt	b. 1981
Genn, Sara	b. 1972	Shaw, Susan	b. 1955
Goldsworthy, Andy	b. 1956	Smith, Bob and Roberta	b. 1963
Gormley, Antony	b. 1950	Smithson, Robert	1938–1973
Himid, Lubaina	b. 1954	Stark, Jen	b. 1983

Useful Organizations and Resources

AccessArt   https://www.accessart.org.uk/

Publishes a range of resources and projects to nurture creativity in the UK.

AEA   **Art Education Australia**   https://www.arteducation.org.au/

Art subject association that provides support, resources and publications for teachers. British writers often contribute articles in the journal *Australian Art Education.*

Big Draw   https://thebigdraw.org/

A pioneering arts education charity dedicated to raising the profile of visual literacy and drawing as a tool for thought, creativity, and social and cultural engagement. Previously known as the Campaign for Drawing, the Big Draw project has become a national festival each year. It publishes a range of materials and resources to aid the exploration of drawing for schools and community groups.

CSEA   **Canadian Society for Education through Art**   https://csea-scea.ca/

Art subject association that provides support, resources and publications for teachers. British writers often contribute articles in the journal *Canadian Art Teacher.*

Engage   **National Association for Gallery Education**   https://www.engage.org/

A society primarily concerned with supporting art gallery educators and promoting learning in galleries. Very helpful resource for locating galleries around the UK. Also publishes a range of materials and an *Engage* journal.

InSEA   **International Society for Education through Art**   http://www.insea.org/

The global voice of art education and official partner of the United Nations Educational, Scientific, and Cultural Organization (UNESCO). It publishes a wide range of materials, magazines, journals, books, etc. It also holds both regional and world congresses where research and current innovative approaches to art education are shared.

NAEA   **National Art Education Association**   https://www.arteducators.org/

US art subject association that provides support, resources and publications for teachers. British writers often contribute articles in the journals *Studies in Art Education* and *Art Education*.

Take one picture   https://www.nationalgallery.org.uk/learning/teachers-and-schools/take -one-picture

A project organized by the National Gallery and used by many schools across the UK. Resources relating to previous years' paintings, and especially the Teachers' Notes, can be downloaded freely from the website. The process is also emulated by several regional galleries and, with some ingenuity, teachers could create their own project having looked at the ways in which this project is constructed.

There is also an inspiring annual exhibition of the work produced by schools at the National Gallery that is well worth visiting.

NSEAD   **National Society for Education in Art and Design**
http://www.nsead.org/home/index.aspx

The UK's art subject association, which provides support, resources and publications for teachers – including through regional networks (details on the website). Teachers also contribute articles in the journals *AD* and *the International Journal for Art and Design Education*.

Room 13 network   http://room13international.org/

As mentioned several times in the book, teachers might like to visit one or more Room 13 projects before considering whether they could host or develop one at their school. The website can be used to locate Room 13s in the UK as well as around the globe. Various other materials and resources can also be found there.

The Fourth Plinth (schools' competition)
https://www.london.gov.uk/what-we-do/arts-and-culture/current-culture-projects/ fourth-plinth-trafalgar-square

The Mayor of London's Office runs an annual competition for schools whereby children can design their own ideas about what should be displayed on the empty plinth in Trafalgar Square. Resources available include a pack for teachers.

Bibliography

Adams, E. (1968), 'Saigon Execution Included in Time 100 Photos'. Available from: www.100photos.time.com [accessed 10 January 2018].

Adams, E. (2001), 'Eulogy', *TIME* Sunday, 24 June 2001. Available from: http://content. time.com/time/magazine/article/0,9171,139659,00.html [accessed January 2018].

Adams, E. (2003a), *Drawing on Experience*. Hove: Drawing Power, The Big Campaign for Drawing.

Adams, E. (2003b), *Power Drawing Notebooks*. Hove: Drawing Power, The Big Campaign for Drawing.

Adams, J. (2005), 'Room 13 and the Contemporary Practice of Artist-Learners', *Studies in Art Education*, 47 (1): 23–33.

Adams, E. (2011), *Drawing It Makes You Think*. Hove: Drawing Power, The Big Campaign for Drawing.

Adams, E. (2016), *Eileen Adams: Agent of Change*. Loughborough: Loughborough Design Press.

Adams, J. N., Worwood, K., Atkinson, D., Dash, P., Herne, S. and Page, T. (2008), *Teaching Through Contemporary Art: A Report on Innovative Practices in the Classroom*. London: Tate Publishing.

Addison, N. (2011), 'Moments of Intensity: Affect and the Making and Teaching of Art', *International Journal of Art and Design in Education*, 30 (3): 363–78.

Addison, N. and Burgess, L. (2002), *Learning to Teach Art and Design in the Secondary School: A Companion to School Experience*. London: Routledge.

Alexander, R. (2006), *Towards Dialogic Teaching: Rethinking Classroom Talk*. Cambridge: Dialogos.

Alexander R. (2009), 'What Is the Primary Curriculum For?' *The Guardian*, 7 April.

Alexander, R. (ed.) (2010), *Children, Their World, Their Education: Final Report and Recommendations of the Cambridge Primary Review*. London: Routledge.

Allen, F. (2011), *Your Sketchbook Your Self*. London: Tate.

Anning, A. and Ring, K. (2004), *Making Sense of Children's Drawing*. New York: Open University Press.

Arnott, C. (2011), 'A Wonder Room, Every School Should Have One', *The Guardian* [online], 31 May. Available from: https://www.theguardian.com/education/2011/may/31/wonder-room-nottingham-university-academy [accessed 20 January 2018]

Arts Council England. (2016), *Art and Design Education, a Guide for Governors and Trustees*. London: Arts Council England.

Barbe-Gall, F. (2005), *How to Talk to Children About Art.*, London: Francis Lincoln.

Barbe-Gall, F. (2012), *How to Talk to Children About Modern Art*. London: Francis Lincoln.

Barnes, R. (2015), *Teaching Art to Young Children*. Oxon: Routledge.

Beetham, H. and Sharpe, R. (2007), *Rethinking Pedagogy for a Digital Age*. Abingdon: Routledge.

Benedict, J. (2001), *Curiosity: A Cultural History of Early Modern Enquiry*. Chicago: Chicago University Press.

Berger, R. (2016), *Austin's Butterfly*. Available from: www.modelsofeducation.org [accessed November 2017].

Big Draw Website. (2016), 'Big Draw'. Available from: https://thebigdraw.org/.

Blackmore, E. and Crowe, M. (2016), 'Staff Audit (for Sheppey Young Arts Advocates Programme)'. Unpublished Audit Report, Eastchurch Church of England Primary School, Eastchurch.

Blakey, S. and McFadyen, J. (2015), 'Curiosity over Conformity: The Maker's Palette – A Case for Hands-On Learning', *Art, Design and Communication in Higher Education,* 14 (2): 131–43.

Bloomfield, A. and Childs, J. (2013), *Teaching Integrated Arts in the Primary School: Dance, Drama, Music and Visual Arts*. London: Fulton.

Bowden, J., Ogier, S. and Gregory, P. (2013), *The Art Subject Leader's Handbook*. London: Belair.

Bradbeer, J., Healey, M. and Kneale, P. (2004), 'Undergraduate Geographers' Understandings of Geography, Learning and Teaching', *Journal of Geography in Higher Education*, 28 (1): 17–34.

Brass, E. and Coles, S. (2014), 'Artist Teachers Exchange: Reflections on a Collaborative Sketchbook Project for Secondary School Art Teachers', *International Journal of Art & Design Education*, 33 (3): 365–74.

Broadhead, P. (2006), '*Developing an Understanding of Young Children's Learning through Play: The Place of Observation, Interaction and Reflection*', *British Educational Research Journal*, 32 (2): 191–207.

Bruner, J. (1986), *Actual Minds, Possible Worlds*. Cambridge, MA: Harvard University Press.

Carle, E. (2013), *The Artist Who Painted a Blue Horse*. London: Puffin.

Chak, A. (2007), 'Teachers' and Parents' Conceptions of Children's Curiosity and Exploration', *International Journal of Early Years Education*, 15 (2): 141–59.

Chalmers, G. (1999), 'Cultural Colonialism and Art Education: Eurocentric and Racist Roots of Art Education', in R. Mason and D. Boughton (eds), *Beyond Multicultural Art Education: International Perspectives*, 173–83. Berlin: Waxman.

Chambers, E. (2014), *Black Artists in British Art: A History from 1950 to the Present*. London: I.B. Tauris.

Chartered College of Teaching. (n.d.), *Access to Research*. Available from: https://chartered.college/ [accessed January 2018].

China, D. (n.d.), *Assessment in Art and Design – Back to Basics*. Available from: http://danchina.net/resources-for-art-teaching/assessment/ [accessed December 2017].

China, D. and Gast, G. (2014), *The National Curriculum for Art and Design Guidance: EYFS, Primary KS1-2*. Corsham: NSEAD. Available from: www.nsead.org [accessed November 2017].

Claxton, G. (2006), 'Thinking at the Edge: Developing Soft Creativity', *Cambridge Journal of Education*, 3: 351–62.

Clement, R. and Tarr, E. (1992), *A Year in the Art of a Primary School*. Corsham: NSEAD.

Clough, P. (2007), *Sculptural Materials in the Classroom*. London: A and C Black Publishers Limited.

Corden, R. (2000), *Literacy and Learning Through Talk: Strategies for the Primary Classroom*. Buckingham: Open University Press.

Corker, C. (2010), 'An Investigation into the Provision for Art, Craft and Design in Primary Initial Teacher Education'. Unpublished MA diss., University of Roehampton.

Cox, M. (1992), *Children's Drawing*. London: Penguin.

Cox, S. (2005), 'Intention and Meaning in Young Children's Drawing', *International Journal of Art and Design Education*, 24 (2): 115–25.

Cox, S. and Watts, R. (eds) (2007), *Teaching Art and Design,* 3–11. London: Continuum.

Craft, A. (2012). 'Childhood in a Digital Age: Creative Challenges for Educational Futures', *London Review of Education*, 10 (2): 173–90.

Crawford, B. A. (2000), 'Embracing the Essence of Inquiry: New Roles for Science Teachers', *Journal of Research in Science Teaching*, 37 (9): 916–37.

Creative Industries Federation. (2018), *Statistics: Jobs*. Available from: https://www.creative industriesfederation.com/statistics [accessed 6 January 2018].

Cultural Learning Alliance. (2014), *Consultation Report on CFE Research: Arts Subjects at Key Stage 4*. UK: Cultural Learning Alliance (online). Available from: http://www. culturallearningalliance.org.uk/userfiles/CLA_report_GCSE_consultation_Feb_2014.pdf [accessed June 2014].

de Eça, P. (2005), 'Using Portfolios for External Assessment: An Experiment in Portugal', *International Journal of Art and Design in Education*, 24 (2): 209–18.

Department for Children, Schools and Families. (2010), *The National Curriculum Primary Handbook*. London: DCSF.

Department for Education. (1995), *Art in the National Curriculum*. London: HMSO.

Department for Education. (2013), *The National Curriculum in England*. London: Department for Education.

Department for Education and Employment. (1999), *All Our Futures: Creativity, Culture and Education*. London: DfEE.

Department of Education and Science. (1992), *Art in the National Curriculum (England)*. London: HMSO.

Dewey, J. (1934), *Art as Experience*. New York: Penguin.

Dowling, M. (2005), *Young Children's Personal, Social and Emotional Development*. London: Paul Chapman.

Downing, D., Johnson, F. and Kaur, S. (2003), *Saving a Place for the Arts? A Survey of the Arts in Primary Schools in England*. Slough: National Foundation for Educational Research (NFER).

Dukas, H. and Hoffmann, B. (eds) (1979), *Albert Einstein, the Human Side: Glimpses from His Archives*. Oxon: Princeton University Press.

Edwards, D. (2010), *The Lab: Creativity and Culture*. Cambridge, MA: Harvard University Press.

Edwards, J. (2013), *Teaching Primary Art*. London: Pearson.

Eglington, K. A. (2003), *Art in the Early Years*. London: RoutledgeFalmer.

Eisner, E. (1997), *Educating Artistic Vision*. New York: Macmillan.

Eisner, E. (2002), *The Arts and the Creation of Mind*. New Haven: Yale University Press.

Eisner, E. (2005), 'Reimaging Schools', in *The Selected Works of Elliot. W. Eisner*. Oxon: Routledge.

Expert Subject Advisory Group (ESAG). (2014). *Art and Design Audit Tool*. Available from: www.esag4art.com [accessed July 2016].

Fisher, R. (2005), *Teaching Children to Think*. Cheltenham: Nelson Thornes.

Fisher, R. (2013), *Teaching Thinking*. London: Bloomsbury.

Fiorani, F. (1998), 'Reviewing Bredecamp 1995', *Renaissance Quarterly*, 51 (1) (Spring): 268–70, p. 268.

Freedman, K. (1994), 'Interpreting Gender and Visual Culture in Art Classrooms', *Studies in Art Education*, 35 (3): 157–70.

Gandini, L. (ed.) (2005), *In the Spirit of the Studio*. New York: Teachers College Press.

Gardner, H. (1990), *Art Education and Human Development*. Los Angeles: Getty Publications.

Garner, S. (2008), *Writing on Drawing: Essays on Drawing Practice and Research*. Chicago: Intellect Books.

Gast, G. (2014), 'Effective Questioning and Talking', NSEAD. Available from: www.nsead. org [accessed 10 November 2017].

Genn, S. (2014), *Eleven Steps to Your World*. Available from: http://painterskeys.com/eleven-steps/ [accessed 17 October 2017].

Gerrard, N. (2017), 'Art Can Be a Powerful Medicine Against Dementia', *The Observer*, 16 July.

Giudici, C. and Vecchi, V. (2004), *Children, Art, Artists*. Reggio Emilia: Reggio Children Publishers.

Gibb, C. (2012), 'Room 13: The Movement and International Network', *International Journal of Art and Design in Education*, 31 (3): 237–44.

Gopaul, E. (2017), *Teaching Primary Art and Design*. London: Bloomsbury.

Gray, P. (2013), *Free to Learn: Why Unleashing the Instinct to Play Will Make Our Children Happier, More Self-Reliant, and Better Students for Life*. New York: Basic Books.

Green, L. and Mitchell, R. (1997), *Art 7–11: Developing Primary Teaching Skills*. London: Routledge.

Greene, M. (1995), *Releasing the Imagination: Essays on Education, the Arts and Social Change*. San-Francisco: Jossey-Bass Education.

Gregory, P. (2005), 'A Deserved Experience!' *Journal of European Teacher Education Network*, 1 (2): 15–24.

Gregory, P. (2006), 'Key Characteristics of Behaviourist and Constructivist Teachers of Art'. Unpublished EdD assignment, University of Greenwich.

Gregory, P. (2013), 'Should Children Be Learning to Make Art or Learning Through Art', in M. Sangster (ed.), *Developing Teacher Expertise: Exploring Key Issues in Primary Practice*, 87–90. London: Bloomsbury.

Gregory, P. (2014), 'An Investigation into the Contribution Made by Primary Art Coordinators to the Development of the Teaching of Art: The Evolution of Identities, Understanding and Practice', EdD thesis, University of Greenwich.

Gregory, P. (2015), 'How Can "Seeing", "Knowing" and "Believing" Impact on Learning in Art and Design', in M. Sangster (ed.), *Challenging Perceptions in Primary Education: Exploring Issues in Practice*. London: Bloomsbury.

Gregory, P. (2016), *A Personal Journey in Art Education: Passions and Reflection*. Available from: http://generationart.gallery/essays/a-personal-journey-in-art-education-passions -and-reflection/

Gregory, P. (2017a), 'Laying Good Foundations? The Value of Art in the Primary School', in R. Mateus-Berr and L. Reitstatter (eds), *Art and Design Education in Times of Change*, 103–7. Berlin: Walter de Gruyter.

Gregory, P. (2017b), 'What's OUR Role in Defining the Future of Art and Design Education?' Keynote presented at NSEAD/IEAADE Conference, Belfast, April 2017.

Gregory, P. (2017c), 'How Long Does It Take to Train a Teacher in Art and Design?' *International Journal of Education in Art and Design (iJADE)*, 36 (2): 130–3.

Gregory, P. (2018), 'Developing Competent Teachers of Art', in R. Hickman (ed.), *International Encyclopaedia of Art and Design Education*. Oxford: Wiley-Blackwell.

Gregory, P. and March, C. (2016), *Art Up on the Downs: New Experiences*. Canterbury: Canterbury Christ Church University.

Gregson, M. (2012), 'Learning Under the Artsmark Umbrella', *Primary Teacher Update*, 2012 (15): 36–8.

Gualtieri, S. (2018), *Facebook Comment*. Available from: https://www.facebook.com/search/ str/remida+reggio+emilia [accessed 30 January 18].

The Guardian. (2015), 'The Secret Teacher', 16 May. Available from: https://www.theguard ian.com/teacher-network/2015/may/16/secret-teacher-sats-stress-childrens-love-of-lear ning.

Hafeli, M. (2014), *Exploring Studio Materials: Teaching Creative Art Making to Children*. New York: Oxford University Press.

Hallam, J., Das Gupta, M. and Lee, H. (2008), 'An Exploration of Primary School Teachers' Understanding of Art and the Place of Art in the Primary School Curriculum', *Curriculum Journal*, 19 (4): 269–81.

Hawkins, H. (2011), 'Dialogues and Doings: Sketching the Relationships between Geography and Art', *Geography Compass*, 57: 464–78.

Herne, S. (2000), 'Breadth and Balance? The Impact of the National Literacy and Numeracy Strategies on Art in the Primary School', *International Journal of Art and Design in Education*, 19 (2): 217–23.

Herne, S. (2007), 'The Subject of Art and Design', in S. Cox and R. Watts (eds), *Teaching Art and Design 3-11*, 1–8. London: Continuum.

Hewlett, C. and March, C. (2016), 'An Introduction to Art and Design', in P. Driscoll, A. Lambirth and J. Roden (eds), *The Primary Curriculum: A Creative Approach*, 2nd ed., 176–94. London: Sage.

Hickman, R. (2005), *Why We Make Art and Why It Is Taught*. Bristol: Intellect.

Hickman, R. (2011), *The Art and Craft of Pedagogy*. London: Bloomsbury.

Hope, G. (2008), *Thinking and Learning through Drawing*. London: Sage.

Hopper, G. (2007), 'Assessment of Art and Design in the Primary School', in T. Rayment (ed.), *The Problem of Assessment in Art and Design*, 27–39. Bristol: Intellect.

Hopper, G. (2015), *Art, Education and Gender: The Shaping of Female Ambition*. London: Palgrave Macmillan.

Horn, S. (2006), 'Inspiration into Installation: An Exploration of Contemporary Experience through Art', *International Journal of Art and Design in Education*, 25 (2): 134–46.

House, R. (ed.) (2011), *Too Much, Too Soon*. Stroud: Hawthorn Press.

Hoye, L. (1998), 'Let's Look at It Another Way: A Constructivist View of Art Education', in L. Huxford and M. Littledyke (eds), *Teaching the Primary Curriculum for Constructive Learning*. London: Fulton.

Huxford, L. and Littledyke, M. (eds) (1998), *Teaching the Primary Curriculum for Constructive Learning*. London: Fulton.

Huxley, E. (2017), 'What Is the Impact of Effective Leadership of Art?' in J. Shearman and P. Gregory (eds), *Leading Success: Leading through a Deep Understanding of Learners in Medway Schools*, 26–30. Canterbury: Canterbury Christ Church University.

Janes, K. (2014), *Using the Visual Arts for Cross-Curricular Teaching and Learning: Imaginative Ideas for the Primary School*. Oxon: Routledge.

Jennings, G. (2006), *Assessment for Learning in Art*. Available from: www.mrjennings.co.uk [accessed December 2017].

Jennings, G. (2014), *Art and Design: Pupil Progress and Target Sheets/Achievement Profile*. Available from: www.mrjennings.co.uk [accessed December 2017].

Key, P. and Stillman, J. (2009), *Teaching Primary Art and Design*. Exeter: Learning Matters.

Klee, F. (ed.) (1960), *Gedichte: Poems by Paul Klee*, trans. M. Wasserman. Montana: Mountain Bridge Press.

Kolbe, U. (2001), *Rapunzel's Supermarket*. Australia: Peppinot.

Lancaster, J. (ed.) (1987), *Art, Craft and Design in the Primary School*. Corsham: NSEAD.

Leslie, I. (2014a), 'The Importance of Encouraging Curiosity in Young Children', *The Guardian*, 7 June.

Leslie, L. (2014b), *Curious*. London: Quercus.

Litman, J., Hutchins, T. and Russon, R. (2005), 'Epistemic Curiosity, Feeling-of-Knowing, and Exploratory Behaviour', *Cognition and Emotion*, 19 (4): 559–82.

Lowenfeld, G. (1994), 'The Psychology of Curiosity: A Review and Reinterpretation', *Psychological Bulletin,* 116 (1): 75–98.

Macdonald, S. (2004), *The History and Philosophy of Art Education*, 3rd edn. Cambridge: Lutterworth Press.

McFall, M. (2013), 'A Cabinet of Curiosities: the little book of awe and wonder', Carmarthen: Independent Thinking Press.

Malin, H. (2013), 'Making Meaningful: Intention in Children's Art Making', *International Journal of Art and Design in Education*, 32 (1): 6–17.

March, C. (March 2016), 'How Can the Sketchbook Support the Development of the Child's Thinking Skills?' Unpublished MA diss., University of Roehampton.

Margolin, V. and Buchanan, R. (eds) (1995), *The Idea of Design*. Bristol: Intellect.

Matthews, J. (2003), *Drawing and Painting: Children and Visual Representation*. London: Paul.

McWilliam, A. (2008), 'Developing an Environmental Aesthetic: Aesthetics and the Outdoor Experience', in G. Coutts and T. Jokela (eds), *Art, Community and Environment*, 30–49. Bristol: Intellect.

Meager, N. (2012), *Teaching Art 4–7*. London: Belair.

Merchant, G. (2012), 'Mobile Practices in Everyday Life: Popular Digital Literacies and Schools Revisited', *British Journal of Educational Technology*, 43 (5): 770–82.

Merchant, G. (2015), 'Keep Taking the Tablets; Ipads, Story Apps and Early Literacy', *Australian Journal of Language and Literacy*, 38 (1): 3–11.

Middleton, I. (2005), 'Foreword: HMI', in T. Wilson (ed.), *Art and Design in Suffolk: Key Stages 1&2*. Ipswich: Suffolk.

Nelson, J. and O'Beirne, C. (2014), *Using Evidence in the Classroom: What Works and Why? Research Summary*. Slough: NFER.

NSEAD. (2014a), *A Manifesto for Art, Craft and Design Education*. Corsham: NSEAD.

NSEAD. (2014b), *Art and Design Programme of Study*. Corsham: NSEAD. Available at www.nsead.org [accessed 12 May 2016].

NSEAD. (2016), *NSEAD Survey*. Corsham: NSEAD. Available from: www.nsead.org [accessed 12 May 2016].

NSEAD / Arts Council England. (2016), *Guidance for School Governors and Trustees*. Corsham: NSEAD. Downloaded from www.nsead.org [accessed January 2017].

Ofsted. (2003), *Good Assessment Practice in Art and Design*. London: Ofsted.

Ofsted. (2008), *Assessment for Learning: The Impact of National Strategy Support*. London: Ofsted.

Ofsted. (2009), *Drawing Together: Art, Craft and Design in Schools (2005–8)*. London: Ofsted.

Ofsted. (2012), *Making a Mark: Art, Craft and Design in Schools (2008–11)*. London: Ofsted.

Ofsted. (2014), *Expectations in Art, Craft and Design: Inspection Guidance Notes for Non-specialist Inspectors*. London: Ofsted.

Ogier, S. (2017), *Teaching Primary Art and Design*. London: Sage.

Ostroff, W. (2016), *Cultivating Curiosity in K-12 Classrooms*. Alexandria: ASCD Publishing.

Oxford Dictionaries. (2011), 12th edn. Oxford: Oxford University Press.

Oxford Road Community School. (2016), https://oxfordroad.reading.sch.uk/.

Page, T., Herne, S., Dash, P., Charman, H., Atkinson, D. and Adams, J. (2006), 'Teaching Now with the Living: A Dialogue with Teachers Investigating Contemporary Art', *International Journal of Art and Design Education*, 25 (2): 146–55.

Pataky, G. (2018), 'The Development of Plastic Art Skills from the Ages of 3 to 7 in Comparison of Two-Dimensional and Three Dimensional Artworks'. Paper presented at the European Network for Visual Literacy (ENViL) Conference, ESPE, Paris, March 2018

Patterson, J. and Roberts, A. (2015), 'Providing Space for Wonder: Fostering Children's Natural Sense of Inquiry', *Questioning for Learning*, 11 (1): 187–200.

Perry, G. (2016), *Sketchbooks*. London: Pengiun London .

Peterson, C. and Seligman, M. (2004), *Character Strengths and Virtues: A Handbook and Classification*. Oxford: Oxford University Press.

Phillips, R. (2014), 'Space for Curiosity', *Progress in Human Geography*, 38 (4): 493–512.

Prentice, R. (ed.) (1995). *Teaching Art and Design*. London: Cassell.

Qualification and Curriculum Agency. (1999), *The National Curriculum: Handbook for Primary Teachers in England*. London: QCA.

Qualification and Curriculum Agency. (2006), *Teacher Assessment Activities Art and Design KS1 and 2*. London: QCA.

Read, H. (1943). *Education through Art*. London: Faber

Rinalda, C. (2006). *Crossing Boundaries: Ideas and Experiences in Dialogue for a New Culture of Education and Adults*. Bergamo : Edizioni Junior, Reggio Children.

Robinson, G. (1993). 'Tuition or Intuition? Making Sketchbooks with a Group of Ten-Year-Olds in the Ordinary Classroom', in S. Herne, S. Cox and R. Watts (eds), *Primary Art Education*. Bristol: Intellect, 2009.

Robinson, G. (1995), *Sketchbook: Explore and Store*. London: Hodder.

Robinson, G., Mountain, A. and Hulston, D. (2011), *Think Inside the Sketchbook*. London: Collins Education.

Robinson, K. (1989), *The Arts 5–16 Practice and Innovation*. Oliver and Boyd.

Rogers, R. (2003), *Time for the Arts?: The Arts in the Initial Training of Primary Teachers: A Survey of Training Providers in England*. West Midlands: Wednesbury Education Action Zone.

Rogoff, I. (2000), *Terra Infirma: Geography's Visual Culture*. London: Routledge.

Roland, C. (2001). 'New Directions for the 21st Century: Technology and Curriculum Design', in D. B. Herberholz (ed.), *Art Works for Elementary Teachers*, 132–40. New York, NY: McGraw Hill.

Rowling, J. K. (2016), *Fantastic Beasts and Where to Find Them*. London: Bloomsbury.

Rowntree, J. and Hooson, D. (2018), *Clay in Common*. Axminster: Triarchy Press.

Rutland, M. (2009), 'Art and Design and Design and Technology: Is There Creativity in the Designing?' *Design and Technology Education*, 14 (1): 56–67.

SCAA. (1997), *Expectations in Art at Key Stages 1 and 2*. London: SCAA.

Shonstrom, E. (2014), 'How Can We Foster Curiosity in the Classroom?' *Education Week*, 33 (33): 22–3.

Smith, K. (2011), 'Curiositas and Studiositas: Investigating Student Curiosity and the Design Studio', *International Journal of Art and Design Education*, 30 (2): 161–75.

Stevenson, A. (ed.) (2010), *Oxford English Dictionary*, 3rd edn. Oxford: Oxford University Press.

Strauss, D. and Gregory, P. (2017), 'Creativity: Thinking and Innovation for Learning and Teaching', in C. Ritchie (ed.), *Understanding Children's Learning*. London: Routledge.

Strong-Wilson, T. and Ellis, J. (2007), 'Children and Place: Reggio Emilia's Environment as Third Teacher', *Journal of Theory into Practice*, 46 (1): 40–7.

Tharp, T. (2008), *Acceptance Speech*, The Nevada Ballet Theatre, 'Woman of the Year Award 2008', Black & White Ball, Wynn Las Vegas, Latour Ballroom, 31 January 2008.

Toogood, C. (2004), *Your Brain on the Page*, Education Tate Britain.

Tutchell, S. (2014), *Young Children as Artists*. Oxon: Routledge.

Tutchell, S. and Vinney, M. (2016), 'Playful Provocations: A Collaborative Dialogue through Drawing'. Paper presented at the International Journal for Art and Design in Education Conference, University of Chester, November 2016.

Tutchell, S. and Witt, S. (2015), 'Confluence; Where Art and Geography Meet'. Paper presented at the Annual RKE Symposium, University of Winchester, April 2015.

Von Renesse, C. and Volker, E. (2017), 'Teaching Inquiry with a Lens Toward Curiosity', *PRIMUS*, 27 (1): 148–64.

Vygotsky, L. (1972). 'The Psychology of Art', *Journal of Aesthetics and Art Criticism*, 30 (4): 564–66.

Wagner, E. and Schönau, D. (eds) (2016), *Common European Framework of Reference for Visual Literacy*. Münster: Waxmann.

Wagner, T. and Compton, R. (2012), *Creating Innovators: The Making of Young People Who Will Change the World*. New York: Scribner.

Ward, H. and Roden, J. (2016), *Teaching Science in the Primary Classroom*. London: Sage.

Watts, A. (2011), *Every Nursery Needs a Garden*. Oxon: Routledge.

Wenham, M. (2003), *Understanding Art: A Guide for Teachers*. London: Paul Chapman.

Wilson, T. (2005), *Art and Design in Suffolk: Key Stages 1 and 2*. Ipswich: Suffolk County Council.

Wilson, T. (2007), *Art in the Early Years*. Ipswich: Suffolk.

Wood, J. (2004), 'Open Minds and a Sense of Adventure: How Teachers of Art and Design Approach Technology', *International Journal of Art and Design Education*, 23 (2): 179–91.

Wright, S. (2010), *Understanding Creativity in Early Childhood*. London: Sage.

Yason, H. (2015), 'The Drawing Room', *AD Magazine (NSEAD)*.

Zion, M. and Slezak, M. (2005). 'It Takes Two to Tango: In Dynamic Inquiry, the Self-Directed Student Acts in Association with the Facilitating Teacher', *Teaching and Teacher Education*, 21: 875–94.

Index